CRYSTAL G
CLAIRV

A practical and theoretical guide to the ancient art or
divination by crystal, including an essay on hygienic
clairvoyance, or the ability to diagnose and prescribe
for disease.

CRYSTAL GAZING
AND
CLAIRVOYANCE

by
JOHN MELVILLE

THE AQUARIAN PRESS LIMITED
Wellingborough, Northamptonshire

First Aquarian Press edition 1979
Fourth Impression 1985

ISBN 0 85030 216 1

Printed and bound in Great Britain

PREFACE.

THE revived interest in the ancient art of Crystal-Divination, the curiosity evinced wherever a translucent sphere or ovoid is exposed to observation, whether in private hands or more public places, and the generally prevailing difficulty of supplying to numerous enquirers, or purchasers of crystals, an answer in concise form to their varied queries arising from generally prevailing lack of information regarding this fascinating subject, have prompted the production of this handbook. The author, while aware of the difference of opinion the issue of this work may produce, ventures notwithstanding to respectfully set forth what he deems a novel hypothesis touching the causes operating to produce the observed phenomena, and the statement of which he is not without hope may lead to further careful research by those into whose hands this little guide may fall.

The tenets of Phrenology and Astrology have both been laid under brief contribution; not that these sciences are necessarily connected, but because it appears to the author wiser to neglect nothing calculated to shed any new light upon an ancient subject.

A partly rewritten abridgment of Jacob Dixon's *" Hygienic Clairvoyance"* has been appended.

That this outline of the occult arts of Crystal-Gazing and Clairvoyance may prove helpful, interesting, and suggestive to the practical experimenter is the desire of the author,

JOHN MELVILLE.

CRYSTAL-GAZING.

THE name Crystal is from the Greek κρύσταλλος, meaning "clear ice," or "frozen water." A crystal is a natural inorganic solid, bounded by plane surfaces, which are symmetrically arranged around certain imaginary lines called axes.

It was thought for many centuries that *rock-crystal* was *water* turned to stone, and this conception remained unchanged until the commencement of the seventeenth century. The term has since been rather loosely applied to any solid capable of assuming geometrical shape under the control of the natural laws; but the crystal which has ever found most favour for the purposes of "crystallomancy," or divination through the medium of "crystal-gazing" is the *Beryl* (Gr. Βήρυλλος.), a mineral (silicate of beryllia), which crystallises in six-sided prisms, the sides of which are often striated longitudinally, but the terminating planes are usually, though not always, smooth. The precious stones known as AQUAMARINE — *sea-green* or sky-blue in colour—the golden beryl, and deep rich green known as the EMERALD, are all *varieties* of the BERYL.

According to Mohs, their *hardness* varies from 7·5 to 8·0, and the *specific gravity* from 2·678 to 2·732.

With an admixture of borax or soda, the beryl forms a beautiful clear glass. The "*Chrysoprasus*" of the Scriptures (more green than the ordinary beryl), and also the *chryso-berylus* (yellowed) and *chrysolithus*, which last was believed to be connected with sight, appear to have been names applied to *different shades* of Beryl, of which Gorraeus gives a list of eight.

BERYL.

According to Gmelin, the chemical composition of the Beryl is as follows :—

Silica	...	...	...	68·07 per cent.
Alumina	...	...	...	17·06 „
Glucina	...	...	...	13·04 „
Red Oxide of Iron	...	0·24 „

The finest come from Dauria on the frontiers of China, from Siberia, and Brazil. One found in the U.S.A. measured :—

$32 \times 22 \times 15$ inches, and weighed 2,900 lbs.
Another, $12 \times 24 \times 45$ inches, and weighed 1,076 lbs.

The stone is called by the Italians, "*Beryl-crystal*," but the English lapidaries drop the use of the latter word, and simply call it "Beryl." It *expands* by heat in a direction *perpendicular* to the principal axis, and *contracts* on the line of the axis; hence there is a point where the expansion and contraction exactly neutralise each other.

The Beryl is harder than ordinary quartz.

Those who may care to study the question of the physiological relation of the eyes to the phenomena of refraction, are referred to the following works :—

"Anomalies of Accommodation and Refraction." Donders. (1864.)
Philosophical Transactions. Thos. Young. (1801.)
Archives of Ophthalmology. Vol. ix., p. 29.

Anomal. d. Refraction. Nagel. P. 461.

Art. Dioptrik des Auges (Listing), in Wagner's " *Handworterbuch der Physiologie.*" (1853.)

Gründzuge der phys. Optik, in vol. ii. of Graefe's " *Handb. der gesammten.*" (1876.)

Other authors are Helmholtz, Brewster, Hermann, Jaeger, Budge, Faraday, etc.

It may be of interest to remark that Dr. J. Pell, an old writer, states that *spectacles* were originally made with the *beryl*-crystal, and that the Germans call a spectacle-glass " *brill* " (beryl) on that account.

Chaucer, in " *The House of Fame*" (b. iii.), mentions the *beryl* thus :—

> " And I amused a long while
> Upon this wall of *berile*,
> That *shone brighter* than a glass,
> And made well more than it was."

According to *Pliny* and *Vossius*, the name is of Eastern origin (cf. Arab, *billaur*, or *ballúr*=crystal). The *beryl* is mentioned in the Bible (A.V.), Rev. xxi. 20.

It may interest the reader to note the respective difference existing between the chemical composition of the ordinary Beryl and the Emerald :—

	Beryl.		Emerald.
Silica	67·00	......	68·50
Alumina ...	16·50	......	15·75
Glucina	14·50	......	12·50
Oxide of Iron	1·00	......	1·00
Oxide of Chromium	0·00	......	0·30
Lime	0·50	......	0·25

The crystal-gazers of the fifth century were known as the *Specularii,* and were established in Ireland.

Saint Augustine believed, and probably with truth, that the practice originated in Persia.

Aubrey in his "*Miscellanies*," pp. 131, etc. (1671), refers to the crystal used in divination as having in its composition "a weak tincture of red" (iron), and quotes a work thereon by Sam Boisardus, entitled, "*De Divinatione per Crystallum.*"

St. Thomas Aquinas, Maury in his "*La Magie et l'Astrologie*," Allan Kardec, and many other writers refer to this art.

In recent years the subject has likewise received attention at the hands of A. E. Waite, Binet et Féré, Mr. F. W. H. Myers, of the London Psychical Research Society, and by Miss X., the well-known writer in "*Borderland*," a quarterly journal of occultism edited by Mr. W. F. Stead; while the "Proceedings of the Psychical Research Society," London, part xiv., for May, 1889, and likewise part xxiii. of the same publication, deal with various facts, theories, or experiments relative to the subject.

THE CRYSTAL.

Pliny, the historian, remarks that it is not easy to say why the crystal takes up the hexagonal form, and particularly mentions that the *points* do not present the same appearance (*eo magis quod neque mucronibus eadem species est*).

"No artist can equal the actual polish of the sides of the crystal," he tells us, and uses the name crystal to indicate the ice-like *transparency* and purity of the stone. He (Pliny) mentions the crystal as having been brought originally from India, and considered it to result from the concretion of water by cold (xxxvii. 2). In this opinion he was supported by Seneca (*Quaest. Nat.* iii. 25), and by Isodorus (*Orig.* xvi. 13). Diodorus Siculus (*Bib.* ii. 134), however, considered it to have been caused *not* by *cold*, but by *fire*.

Amongst the Fathers of the Church, Austin, Jerome, Isidore, Basil, and Gregory the Great, held the views of Pliny. Sir Thomas Brown, in his "*Enquiry into Common Errors*," denies the philosophy of the ancients.

Nicolaus Stena, born at Copenhagen, Denmark, in 1638, in his treatise, "*De solida intra solidum naturaliter contenta*" (1669), rejects *extreme cold* as being the *cause* of crystallisation, and attributed the latter to *magnetic power*, or something akin thereto. He considered that crystals grew, not from within, but from without, through the medium of infinitesimal particles carried to, and deposited definitely at the *ends* of the crystal; while he likewise held them to manifest the phenomena of *continued growth.* He laid it down as his conviction " that the number and length of the sides in the plane of the axis may vary widely without change in the angles" (*in plano axis, literum et numerum et longitudinem varie multari non mutatis angulis*).

Many other observers and writers may be mentioned, among whom are Leeuwenhoek in his "*Arcana Naturæ*" (1695), Sir Isaac Newton in " *Optics* " (1706), Englielmini in " *De Salibus Dissertatio Epistolaris* " (1707), Robert Boyle, De la Hire, Cappeller, and Henckel, in whose various writings many curious and interesting observations relative to the subject may be found.

Linnaeus, who also wrote upon crystallography, gave an impetus to the investigations of Romé Delisle, whose able

"*Essai de Crystallographie*" appeared in **1772**, and was followed eleven years later by an enlarged edition, in which he gives upwards of five hundred regular forms of crystals, while at the same time affirming "*that, amidst all the innumerable variations of which the primitive form of a crystal is susceptible, there is* ONE THING *that* NEVER VARIES, *and remains constantly the same in each species—viz., the angle of incidence, or the respective inclination of the faces to each other.*"

The name *crystal* was *originally* applied only to ordinary quartz, or "rock-crystal." The Italians spoke of it as "*cristalla*," the Spanish "*cristal*," the French "*crystal*," Latin "*crystallus*." Later on, the term was more *generally* applied to any symmetrically formed mineral, solid, transparent, or opaque, contained or bounded by plane surfaces. Ben Jonson mentions the existence of crystal divination and its accompaniments thus :—

> "They have their *chrystals*, I do know, and *rings*,
> And *virgin parchment*, and their dead men's skulls,
> Their raven wings, their *lights*, and *pentacles*,
> With characters ; I ha seen all these."
>
> 　　　　　　　　　　　　(*Devil an Ass.*, i., 2.)

Swedborg, in his "Earths in the Universe" (Lond., 1860) p. 7, speaking of the inhabitants of the planet *Mercury*, says :—

> "Some of them are desirous to appear, not like the spirits of other earths, as men, but as *crystalline globes*. Their desire to appear so, although they do not, arises from the circumstance that the *knowledges of things immaterial* are in the other life *represented by crystals*."

In the United Kingdom beryl is found among the Mourne Mountains, Co. Down ; in the neighbourhood of Killiney,

Co. Dublin; in Co. Wicklow; in some parts of Cornwall; and in Aberdeenshire in the granite of Rubislaw, and also in the upper reaches of the Dee and the Don. It occurs likewise in Rio San Matteo in Brazil, Schlackenwald in Bohemia, in Siberia, and many other parts, such as New Hampshire, Massachusetts, Maine, Connecticut, etc., U.S.A. Occurring thus in great abundance, it has comparatively depreciated in value; but amongst the Romans it was highly prized in the manufacture of jewellery. Mount Zabarah, in Upper Egypt, was the probable source from which the ancients derived the beryl. The colours of the beryl range from blue through honey-yellow to absolute transparency; the latter resulting from the presence of peroxide of iron, while the green and various shades of blue represent the effect of protoxide of iron in varying quantities. The favourite shade of this crystal utilised by ancient Seers was the pale water-green beryl or delicate "aquamarine"—the same referred to by Drayton in his *Nymphal* 9, thus :—

> "The topaz we'll stick here and there,
> And *sea-green coloured beryl.*"

For the use of this hue, or tint, there appears to have been more than one reason. Certainly other stones, such as the white sapphire, and even vessels of water, were pressed into the service; but it must be remembered that water-green was, astrologically considered (and all divination was more or less connected with high astrology), a colour especially under the influence of the MOON, an orb exerting very great *magnetic* influence.

Now, when we, in the first place, reflect that the *Beryl,*

Emerald, Sapphire, Adamantine Spar, etc., *all contain Oxide of Iron,* a substance presenting the strongest affinity for *Magnetism,* and when we also remember the *strict injunctions* of the ancient occultists to utilise the Crystal *only during the increase* of the *Moon,* the idea naturally suggests itself that the connecting link between the crystal and the spiritual world is MAGNETISM, attracted to and accumulated in or around the Crystal by the *iron* infused throughout its constitution, and that the *greater the increase of the Moon* the greater consequently is *the supply and accumulation of the Lunar magnetism in the crystal.*

This theory is strengthened by the statements of P. B. Randolph, the occultist, who, writing of the manufacture of *magic mirrors,* informs us that the *great desideratum* is to *retain* the accumulated *magnetism* upon the surface of the mirrors, and it is the difficulty of achieving this which renders the production of genuine mirrors so costly.

But granted that the above-mentioned theory be correct in relation to the crystal itself, the further question naturally arises—How is the operator placed *en rapport* with the crystal globe, sphere, or ovoid ; or, in other words, what is the secret or *modus operandi* of bringing the inquirer or experimenter into direct contact with the crystal, and, through its medium, with the unseen world ? To this question we render the following reply :—

(a) By CONCENTRATION in the CRYSTAL of the greatest possible influx of celestial or terrestrial magnetism, or both.

(b) By CONCENTRATION in the BODY of the operator of unalloyed magnetism, through the purity of the amatory functions.

(c) By CONCENTRATION of the MIND, through the mental faculty of "*Concentrativeness*," acting through the Phrenological Brain "centre," located in the *superior portion* of the *First Occipital convolution* of the Cerebrum.

Hence, those persons endowed with *natural ability* to *concentrate the attention,* are thereby *aided* in their use of the sphere. To what extent this power exists in the would-be experimenter can be told by a first-class Phrenologist.

(d) CONCENTRATION of the GAZE upon the Crystal. Why? Because, as taught by the famous Baron Reichenbach, there streams from the human eyes an efflux of Magnetism, projected from its reservoir in the Cerebellum, when the gaze is concentrated upon a given point.

At this juncture it may be remarked that the "*centres*" *of sight* are located by modern Physiologists in the *posterior lobes* of the Brain, above the region of the Cerebellum.

Now observe :—

(a) That the ancients taught the importance of *strict purity* in relation to the *amatory nature,* when either crystal-gazing, clairvoyance, or other occult efforts were put forth, and hence the use of boys and virgins in crystal-divination.

(b) That Phrenologists have located the propensity to *physical love* in the *Cerebellum,* or small brain, just beneath the before-mentioned posterior lobe of the Cerebrum.

(c) This being so, the *Cerebellum* became, as it were, a *reservoir* of *Magnetism,* directly connected with the *creative* economy, or would at all events *influence* the *quality* of the *magnetic outflow* through the *eyes*—the brain "centres" for which lie just above the region of the Cerebellum, as also does that area devoted to the "*concentration of attention*," as taught by the most modern physiologists such as Prof. Ferrier. (See Plate I.)

The *Cerebellum* is held by various authorities to preside over, or be connected with, the co-ordination of *muscular* movement of the limbs. It is situated in the *inferior occipital fossae* below the *tentorium*. The Phrenologist, while recognising the influence of the Cerebellum over co-ordinated movement, claims certain of its parts as being *also related* to *physical love*, which is in its turn closely *allied* to *muscular action*.

Purity of the *Blood* is important to *purity* of *power*. Hence the life fluid *must be purified*. Food, Digestion, Sleep, Drinks—all must receive a proper degree of attention. Sound physical organs are not absolutely *essential*, but nevertheless it is *best* to enjoy healthy Brain, Heart, Liver, Kidneys, Stomach, Lungs, and pelvic apparatus, if one desires to attain to a *high degree* of *lucidity*, or clearness of mental vision, and all this largely depends upon the condition of the BLOOD. Clairvoyance depends as much upon air, light, diet, sleep, labour, music, health, as upon mechanically induced magnetism, or mesmerism.

The condition of the vital fluid at the time of experimenting with the crystal being of so great importance, it will be of utility for the reader to consider the following facts :—

There is, on an average, one part by weight of *iron* in

two hundred and thirty human blood corpuscles, and the total quantity of iron in the blood of a man weighing one hundred and forty pounds, is about thirty-eight grains, while about one grain per day is on the average taken into the body with food. Iron is a component part of the hæmoglobin of the blood, and forms the colouring matter of the *red* blood corpuscles. The *white* or *colourless corpuscles* which are much fewer in number than the red, in a healthy body are *diminished by Fasting*, and *increased by eating*, and this fact is of interest in connection with the advisability of *fasting prior to magnetic experiment* with the CRYSTAL globe, as enjoyed by the Seers of the past.

Two principal forms of iron are apparent in the blood :—
1. *Protoxide of iron*, which is principally found in the *Venous* or *dark* blood. This is also known as *ferrous oxide*, and constitutes the *base* of the *green* or ferrous salts of iron, which latter cannot be obtained in an isolated state. *Protoxide of iron* combines with water to form a hydrate, FeO, HO, which, on the addition of an alkali, falls in white flakes, provided the water in which they are suspended contains *no free oxygen;* otherwise the precipitate is grey.
2. *Peroxide of iron*, which is mostly found in the *arterial*, or *bright scarlet* blood. It is known as *sesquioxide*, or *ferric oxide*, colcothar, "crocus of Mars," hæmatite, rouge, or red oxide of iron. It is the base of the *red* or ferric salts (Fe_2O_3), and is practically the same thing as iron-rust, which is a hydrated peroxide.

Now, a *compound* of the two preceding oxides constitutes what was formerly known as the "*loadstone*," or black *magnetic* oxide of iron; and it is a remarkable fact that persons of dark or very dark hair, eyes, and skin are the most magnetic; and this darkness is, it would seem, connected with a preponderance of the *protoxide of iron* in the blood over the *peroxide* in the proportion of two (2) parts to one (1), which happens to be a similar proportion to that existing in the "loadstone." Such persons are usually dominantly representative of a *bilious* tendency, or so-called "bilious temperament;" and we know that the amount of *iron* in the *bile* is important, being present as a phosphate derived from hæmoglobin.

Some of the iron is stored in the liver cells, and some discharged as phosphate into the bile, in which latter oxygen is almost wholly absent, though small quantities of nitrogen are found, the most important gas being the carbonic acid.

When we remember the importance of *deep breathing* in clairvoyant effort, the *antibilious* tendency of the "mugwort" and other magnetically inclined herbs, the facts in general seem to point to the conclusion that a *certain chemical balance* between the ferric and oxygenic, and consequently *magnetic* conditions of the BLOOD and BILE, are necessary for the obtainance of the *most perfect* powers of *concentration* and *lucid sight*, or clairvoyance.

Miss X., of "*Borderland*" fame, has stated that in her judgment the phenomena of crystal vision may be classed as follows :—

1. Images of something unconsciously observed. New *reproductions*, voluntary or spontaneous, and *bringing no fresh knowledge* to the mind.

2. Images of *ideas unconsciously acquired from others*, by telepathy or otherwise. Some Memory or Imaginative effect, which does not come from the gazer's ordinary self. *Revivals of Memory.* Illustrations of Thought.

3. Images, clairvoyant or prophetic. *Pictures bringing information* as to something *past, present,* or *future* which the gazer has *no other chance of knowing.*

With this view I cordially agree, and hence would impress upon the reader the fact that *anything* and *everything* perceived in the crystal does *not* belong to the phenomena coming under the *third* heading, *which latter alone* are in the category of *true crystal-divination,* as taught and practised by the ancient Seers.

Such pictures as belong to divisions 1 and 2 may, of course, appear not only in a crystal, but in a vase, glass of water decanter, etc., etc., the mere result of visualisation; and their production requires little or none of the care and observation of conditions herein set forth for the guidance of the more spiritual investigation.

It is clear that the *effects* obtained through the medium of crystal-gazing are *variable* in kind, as before stated. For example :—Scenes or pictures may appear to the gazer which are merely a *reproduction* of those which have been *previously seen,* and impressed upon the vision of the experimenter in much the same manner as upon the mind of the ordinary artist, when he pictures and paints in detail upon his canvas in the studio some scene or landscape memorised by him a week before. Phrenology teaches that this power, which is not confined to artists, but is likewise utilised by mental calculators, detectives, and others, is largely dependent on the faculty of "FORM," whose correspondent brain "centre" is located in the first frontal convolution of the cerebrum, upon the two sides of the "*crista galli.*" Dr. J. F. Gall, the Father of Phrenology, called it "*Aptness to recollect persons.*" It is perceptive and recollective of shape, outline, profile, and contour, and he ce of faces and forms in general.

An individual strongly endowed by nature with this power has, as the *external sign* of the *internal brain form*, the *eyes set widely apart* in the face. Now, where an individual possesses this faculty in marked degree of development, his ability to *reproduce* a bygone scene *before the mental vision*, is very much stronger *involuntarily* than where this sign is lacking; and if, *added to this*, the bodily temperament is of fine sensitive quality, and the faculties of "*Ideality*" (imagination — near the *vertical Frontal fissure*) and "*Spirituality*" (called by Dr. Gall "*organe qui dispose aux visions*"—the organ disposing one to perceive visions, the prophetic instinct—and by Dr. Spurzheim, "*Supernaturalité*," the brain "centre" of ideation, which is located in the "*Ascending Frontal convolution*,") be well or strongly marked in development (phrenological), it is clear that an individual so endowed possesses a far better chance of successfully using the crystal, for the *mere reproduction* of bygone scenes, etc., than has one in whom these endowments are lacking or weakly represented.   (See Plate I.)

The writer suggests that an infusion of the herb *Mugwort* (*artemesia vulgaris*), the properties of which are tonic and *antibilious*, or of the herb *Succory*, would, if taken occasionally during the Moon's increase by the would-be crystal-gazer, constitute an *aid* to the attainment of the most desirable *physical conditions* of the experimenter's body.

The reasons for this suggestion are :—

1. That the constituents of both these plants are specially *responsive* to *magnetic* influence; their leaves, like the compass needle, invariably turning of themselves towards the north.

PLATE I.

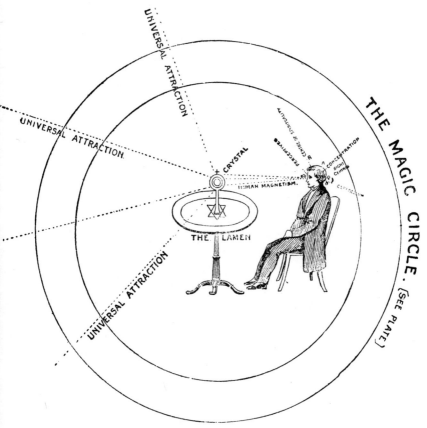

≏ "*Libra*," or the Zodiacal Sign governing the *Perceptive* Faculties over tne *Eyes* and *Kidneys.*

♉ "*Taurus*," or the Zodiacal Sign governing the *Neck* and *Cerebellum* and Amative functions.

☽ "*Luna*," the *Moon*.

♀ Venus.

A Back of the Brain containing "centres" of Sight, "*Concentration of Attention*" and "*Adhesive attraction.*"

B "Centre" of "*Spirituality*" in the Brain.

2. As the BERYL is under the zodiacal sign LIBRA, so also are these herbs.

3. LIBRA is the sign more particularly related to the RENAL or KIDNEY SYSTEM, which latter is in its turn closely connected with—

(a) The PERCEPTIVE Faculties and Brain "centres" of the phrenologists corresponding thereto, and therefore with the EYES (see Plate I.);

(b) With the INTUITIVE powers.

(c) Reference has already been made to the CEREBELLAR or amative relations of the EYES, and power of "Concentration of Attention" in the Brain, and as the zodiacal sign LIBRA is one of the two signs primarily related to VENUS (*Taurus* being the second), who rules the generative and kidney system, the general connection of all the foregoing forces with the subject under consideration—viz., crystal-gazing—will be clearly apparent to the esoteric student. (See Plate I.)

4. That, being *antibilious*, and acting also upon the *generative system*, these herbs influence beneficially the functions most closely allied to magnetic force, acting in conjunction with sensitive intuition, and upon the production of the said force and its constitution.

The following tabulation may aid to render these ideas clearer :—

Zodiacal Signs.	Planet.	Temperament.
1. Libra......	................Hot and Moist—Sanguine.	
	Venus ....Cold and Moist—Lymphatic.	
2. Taurus...	................Cold and Dry—Nervous.	
	Moon ....Cold and Moist—Phlegmatic.	

It will be observed by this table *that neither of the signs or planets, which appear from our analysis to be specially contributory to the lucid powers, are of the pronounced* BILIOUS TEMPERAMENT.   Hence it would seem that the Mugwort and Succory, *being* ANTIBILIOUS, *tend to the preservation* of just those bodily conditions indicated by the above-named temperaments.

Leaving now this theory, let us glance at the connection of the MOON therewith.

According to Astrology the *Crystals* and *Selenite* come under her influence, while the *Intuitive Powers* of the *Mind* and *Brain* are likewise largely affected thereby. Now the Poles of the HUMAN BRAIN specially dominated by the MOON are located (*a*) in the region extending from just above the EYES (the PERCEPTIVES of phrenologists) — an area related to LIBRA, let us remember, as we have already seen—and (*b*) the back of the NECK where it joins the head, the very area ruled by TAURUS, and also containing the phrenological " centres " of amative force in the cerebellum. (See Plate I.)

Due attention should ever be paid to the following principal *Magnetic Laws* :—

1. *Persistence of Purpose* to a given End or Aim.
2. *Attention.*
3. *Calmness.*
4. *Will.*   (The " It-shall-be-as-I-want-it " power.)
5. *Intensity.*
6. *Polarity.*

HINTS ON THE USE OF THE CRYSTAL.

1. Keep the crystal clean. If *very* dirty or discoloured treat it as follows:—Mix together six parts water and one of brandy. Boil them over a brisk fire, and let the crystal be kept in a boiling state about fifteen minutes. Then take out and rub carefully over with a brush dipped in the same liquor. Rub dry with chamois leather.

2. The person *for whom you are going to look,* may hold it in their hands for a few minutes previous to its use, but *no one else,* except yourself.

3. If the crystal appears hazy or dull, it is a sign that you are likely to see; it will afterwards *clear,* and the form or vision become manifest. Immediately before the apparition is beheld, the crystal becomes clouded or darkened, or what some term "black." Presently this clears away, and the crystal becomes exceeding bright, as if illuminated by an effulgence proceeding from its interior, doubtless due to the iron and magnetism disseminated throughout its constitution.

4. If you require to see events taking place at a great distance look *lengthwise* through the crystal.

The works of olden days insist upon elaborate ceremonial as follows :—

(*a*) Use frequent ablutions (washings) and prayers, three or four days before consulting the crystal.

(*b*) The MOON must be in her INCREASE, *i.e.,* going towards the FULL. (This should never be neglected. It is of great importance to your success.)

(*c*) When the SUN is in his greatest Northern declination is the best time, so far as regards his influence in the matter.

(*d*) The room must be clean and neat, with nothing therein likely to disturb the attention, and should be kept locked when not in use.

(*e*) The floor must be well scoured, or clean. Every preparation must be made *during the Moon's increase.*

(*f*) Place in the room a small table, covered with a white linen cloth. (This if the experimenter does not use the ancient *Lamen* or Holy Table.) (See Plate II.)

(*g*) A chair, and materials for a fire. The fire is for burning the usual perfumes.

(*h*) Two wax candles in gilt or brass candlesticks, highly polished ; a pair of compasses ; twine ; knife ; scissors, etc.

The Crystal should be about 1½ inch in *diameter*, or at least the size of a small orange. It should be enclosed in a frame of ivory, ebony, or boxwood, highly polished, or stood upon a glass or crystal pedestal. (See Plate III.)

When following strictly the ancient methods described herein, the Crystal is to be stood upon the Lamen or table, but if simply *held in the hand*, its top end should *lean away* from the gazer, and should be held so that no reflections or shadows appear therein. If stood on the table, the folds of a black silk handkerchief may be arranged about the crystal so as to shut out reflections.

The mystic names to be engraved in raised letters of gold round about the frame, according to some authorities, are:—

On the N.   Tetragrammaton.
    „   E.   Emmanuel.
    „   S.   Agla.
    „   W.   Adonay.

PLATE II.

The Top of the Lamen.

The pedestal which supports the frame should bear **the** mystical name

SADAY;

while on the pedestals of the two candlesticks

ELOHIM and
ELOHE

must be respectively embossed.

In consecrating, the forms must be repeated while the invocant is *laying his hands* upon the different articles. His *face* must be *turned to the* EAST while this is being done.

No crystal or mirror should be handled by other than the owner, because such handling mixes the magnetisms, and tends to destroy their sensitiveness. Others may *look* into them, but should not touch them, except the person who may be consulting the gazer, as already mentioned. If the surface becomes dirty or soiled, it may be cleaned with fine soapsuds, rinsed well, washed with alcohol or vinegar and water, and then polished with soft velvet or a chamois leather.

The crystal or mirror should frequently be magnetised by passes made with the *right hand*, for about five minutes at a time. This *aids* to give it *strength* and *power*. Similar passes with the *left hand* add to the *sensitiveness* of the crystal.

The *back* of the mirror or crystal should be held *toward* the *light*, but its face never.

The *Magnetism* with which the surface of the mirror or crystal becomes charged, *collects there from the eyes of the gazer*, and from the universal ether, the Brain being as it were switched on to the Universe, the crystal being the medium.

Persons of a *Magnetic Temperament*, such as, amongst others, those who are classed as *brunette, dark-eyed, brown-skinned*, and having *dark hair*, will charge the crystal or mirror quicker, but *not more effectually*, than those of opposite or electric temperament, such as the *blonde*.

APPEARANCES IN THE CRYSTAL.

White Clouds - - - indicate	Good ; the affirmative ; favour.
Black Clouds - - - ,,	Bad ; inauspicious.
Violet, Green, Blue - - ,,	Coming joy; excellent.
Red, Crimson, Orange, Yellow ,,	Danger, trouble, sickness; " beware ;" deception, grief, betrayal, slander, loss ; surprises of a disagreeable nature.
Ascending Clouds - - ,,	*Affirmative replies* to questions asked. Yes ! If the *query* is a *silent* one it makes no difference.
Descending Clouds - - ,,	The negation of all questions. No !

Whatever appears on the *left-hand* side of the gazer is *real*, or a picture of an *actual* thing.

Whatever appears on the *right-hand* side is symbolical.

Moonlight	Benefits the mirror or crystal.
Sunlight	The chemical and active rays or influence of the direct *sunlight* are *injurious*, and will ruin the magnetic susceptibility of the crystal.
Extremes of Heat or Cold	Are likewise injurious.
Clouds or Shadows	Moving toward the gazer's *right hand*, indicate the *presence of spiritual beings*, and *their interest.*
Clouds or Shadows	Moving towards the *left hand* mean "The séance is ended for the present time."

WARNING.

A sure and certain law exists, *viz.* :—That if the seer's *purpose* be *evil* when he or she uses the crystal or mirror, it will *react* upon the seer sooner or later *with terrible effect*; wherefore all are strictly cautioned to *be good* and *do good* only.

The aerial spaces are *thronged* with countless intelligences—celestial, *good*, *pure*, *true*, and the *reverse*. The *latter* have FORCE : the *former* possess POWER. To reach the *good ones, the heart of the gazer must correspond*, and they should be invoked with prayerful feelings.

There **are** innumerable multitudes of the *bad* on the confines of *Matter* and *Spirit*. These malign forces are many and terrible; but they can never reach the soul that relies on God in perfect faith, and which only invokes the Good, the Beautiful, and True for noble purposes.

In using the Crystal the Ancients used the following Prayer:—

"O God, who art the Author of all good things, strengthen, I beseech Thee, Thy poor servant, that he may stand fast without fear through this dealing and work; enlighten, I beseech Thee, O Lord, the dark understanding of Thy creature, so that his spiritual eye may be opened to see and know Thy angelic spirits descending here in this Crystal. (Here lay your hand on the Crystal, saying)— And thou, O inanimate creature of God, be sanctified and consecrated and blessed to this purpose, that no evil phantasy may appear in thee; or, if they do gain ingress into this creature, they may be constrained to speak truly, intelligibly, and without ambiguity. For Christ's sake. *Amen.* And forasmuch as Thy servant here standing before Thee, O Lord, desires neither evil, treasures, nor injury to his neighbour, nor hurt to any living creature, grant him the power of descrying those celestial spirits or intelligences that may appear in this Crystal, and whatever good gifts (whether the power of healing infirmities or of imbibing wisdom, or discovering any evil likely to afflict any person or family, or any other good gift Thou mayest be pleased to bestow on me, enable me, by Thy wisdom and mercy, to use whatever I may receive to the honour of Thy Holy Name. Grant this for Thy Son Christ's sake. *Amen.*"

Then, taking the ring and pentacle, put the ring on the

PLATE III.

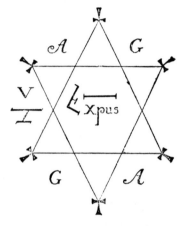

The Crystal, set in pure gold, and stood in the centre of the Lamen, or Holy Table.

The Pentacle of Solomon, as engraved on solid square plate of silver.

AGLA ✡ ON ✡ TETRAGRAMMATON — ✠

The Magic Wand of Black Ebony. Engraven on the opposite side are the words:—
EGO, ALPHA et OMEGA.

little finger of your right hand.   Hang the pentacle (see Plate III.) round your neck.   Then take your black ebony wand (see Plate III.) and trace the *circle*[1] (see Plate IV.), saying :—

"In the name of the blessed Trinity I consecrate this piece cf ground for our defence ; so that no evil spirit may have power to break these bounds prescribed here. Through Christ the Lord. *Amen.*"

Then place the vessel for the *perfumes* between the circle and the holy table, on which the crystal stands, and having fire thereon, cast in the perfumes, saying :—

"I conjure thee, O thou creature of fire, by Him who created all things both in Heaven and Earth, and in the sea, and in every other place whatever, that forthwith thou cast away every phantasm from thee, that no hurt whatsoever shall be done in any thing."

"Bless, O Lord, this creature of fire, and sanctify it, that it may be blessed, and that they may fill up the power and virtue of their odours; so neither the enemy nor any false imagination may enter into them.   Through our Lord Jesus Christ.   *Amen.*"

It does not follow that the same spirit you call will always appear, and you must try the spirit, to know whether he be a pure or impure being, and this you will easily know by a firm and undoubted faith in God. Now, the most pure and simple way of "calling" the spirit or spirits is by a *short oration to the spirit himself.* Therefore, after the circle is drawn, the book, perfumes,

---

[1] The preferable time in which the Circle may be entered by the operator, is in the day and hour of Mercury, the Moon increasing.

rod, etc., in readiness, proceed as follows (after noticing the *exact hour* of the day, and what *angel rules* that hour (see Tables I. and II.), thou shalt say this " Call ") :—

" In the name of the blessed and holy Trinity, I do desire thee, thou strong and mighty angel, *Michael*[1] (see Tables I. and II.), that if it be the divine will of Him who is called Tetragrammaton, etc., the Holy God, the Father, that thou take upon thee some shape, as best becometh thy celestial nature, and appear to us visibly here *in this Crystal*, and answer our demands in as far as we shall not transgress the bounds of the divine mercy and goodness, by requesting unlawful knowledge, but that thou wilt graciously show us what things are most profitable for us to know and do, to the glory and honour of His Divine Majesty, who liveth and reigneth, world without end. *Amen.*"

" Lord, Thy will be done on earth, as it is in heaven. Make clean our hearts within us, and take not Thy Holy Spirit from us."

" O Lord, by Thy name we have called him. Suffer him to administer unto us, and that all things may work together for Thy honour and glory, to whom with Thee, the Son, and blessed Spirit, be ascribed all might, majesty, and dominion. *Amen.*"

Note.—In these dealings *two* should always be present, for often a spirit is manifest to one, in the *crystal*, when the other cannot perceive him ; therefore, if any spirit appear, as is most likely, to one or both, say—

" O Lord, we return Thee our hearty and sincere thanks

---

[1] Or any other angel or spirit. Vassago, the " genius " of the Crystal, was anciently invoked.

PLATE IV.

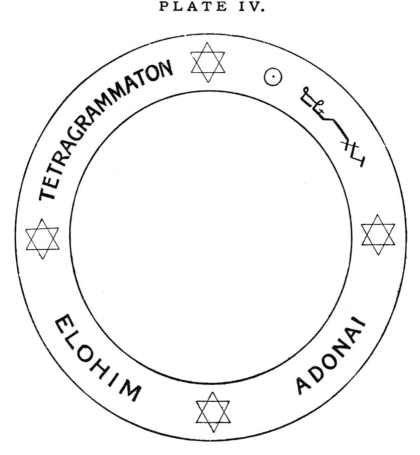

The Magic Circle in which the Lamen and Crystal-gazer stand.

for the hearing of our prayer, and we thank Thee for having permitted Thy spirit to appear unto us, which we by Thy mercy will interrogate to our further instruction. *Amen.*"

Interrogation 1.—In the name of the holy and undefiled Spirit, the Father, the begotten Son, and Holy Ghost (proceeding from both), what is thy true name? (If the spirit answers *"Michael,"* then proceed.)

Interrogation 2.—What is thy office?

Interrogation 3.—What is thy true sign or character?

Interrogation 4.—When are the times most agreeable to thy nature to hold conference with us? Wilt thou swear by the blood and righteousness of our Lord Jesus Christ that thou art truly *Michael?*

(Here let him swear, then write down his seal or character in thy book, and against it, his office, and times to be "called" through God's name; also write down anything he may teach thee, or any *responses* he may make to thy questions or interrogations concerning life and death, arts or sciences, or any other thing.)

Then shalt thou say—

"Thou great and mighty spirit, inasmuch as thou camest in peace and in the name of the ever-blessed and righteous Trinity, so in this name thou mayest depart, and return to us, when we call thee in His name, to whom every knee doth bow down. Fare thee well, *Michael;* peace be between us. Through our blessed Lord Jesus Christ. *Amen.*"

Then will the spirit depart. Then say, "To God the Father, eternal Spirit, fountain of Light, the Son, and Holy Ghost, be all honour and glory, world without end. *Amen.*"

The best times, generally speaking, for using the Crystal are—At Sunrise; at Mid-day; at Sunset. The *worst* are from ten o'clock p.m. to two o'clock a.m.

———

Here we bring to a close this attempt to present the reader with a guide to the art of using the crystal. Much more of an interesting nature, relative to this subject, might have been added, but would be beyond the scope of this handbook. Practical and careful experiment will, if nothing more, be yet found helpful in the direction of *increasing* the power of *mental concentration*, and thus conducing to success in life.

Let us lift up our desires to Him, by whom we are "fearfully and wonderfully made," and echo in our hearts the words of Taylor :—

> " When Thou Thy jewels dost bind up, that day
>   Remember us, we pray.
>   That where the *beryl* lies,
>   And the *crystal* 'bove the skies,
>   There Thou mayest appoint us a place
>   Within the brightness of Thy face ;
>   And our soul
>   In the scroll
>   Of life and blissfulness enroll,
>   That we may praise Thee to eternity."
>   (*The Golden Grove.*)

TABLE showing the respective *Angels* whose names are to be inserted in the Prayer in place of " Michael," according to the hour of day or night when the crystal is used ; and for finding the *Angel* and *Planet* ruling any hour of the *Day* or *Night*.

I.

Hour.	SUNDAY. Day.	MONDAY. Day.	TUESDAY. Day.
1.	☉ Michael.	☽ Gabriel.	♂ Samael.
2.	♀ Anael.	♄ Cassiel.	☉ Michael.
3.	☿ Raphael.	♃ Sachiel.	♀ Anael.
4.	☽ Gabriel.	♂ Samael.	☿ Raphael.
5.	♄ Cassiel.	☉ Michael.	☽ Gabriel
6.	♃ Sachiel.	♀ Anael.	♄ Cassiel
7.	♂ Samael.	☿ Raphael.	♃ Sachiel
8.	☉ Michael.	☽ Gabriel.	♂ Samael.
9.	♀ Anael.	♄ Cassiel.	☉ Michael.
10.	☿ Raphael.	♃ Sachiel.	♀ Anael.
11.	☽ Gabriel.	♂ Samael.	☿ Raphael.
12.	♄ Cassiel.	☉ Michael.	☽ Gabriel.

Hour.	WEDNESDAY. Day.	THURSDAY. Day.	FRIDAY. Day.	SATURDAY. Day.
1.	☿ Raphael.	♃ Sachiel.	♀ Anael.	♄ Cassiel.
2.	☽ Gabriel.	♂ Samael.	☿ Raphael.	♃ Sachiel.
3.	♄ Cassiel.	☉ Michael.	☽ Gabriel.	♂ Samael.
4.	♃ Sachiel.	♀ Anael.	♄ Cassiel.	☉ Michael.
5.	♂ Samael.	☿ Raphael.	♃ Sachiel.	♀ Anael.
6.	☉ Michael.	☽ Gabriel.	♂ Samael.	☿ Raphael.
7.	♀ Anael.	♄ Cassiel.	☉ Michael.	☽ Gabriel.
8.	☿ Raphael.	♃ Sachiel.	♀ Anael.	♄ Cassiel.
9.	☽ Gabriel.	♂ Samael.	☿ Raphael.	♃ Sachiel.
10.	♄ Cassiel.	☉ Michael.	☽ Gabriel.	♂ Samael.
11.	♃ Sachiel.	♀ Anael.	♄ Cassiel.	☉ Michael.
12.	♂ Samael.	☿ Raphael.	♃ Sachiel.	♀ Anael.

II.

Hour.	SUNDAY. Night.		MONDAY. Night.		TUESDAY. Night.	
1.	♃	Sachiel.	♀	Anael.	♄	Cassiel.
2.	♂	Samael.	☿	Raphael.	♃	Sachiel.
3.	☉	Michael.	☽	Gabriel.	♂	Samael.
4.	♀	Anael.	♄	Cassiel.	☉	Michael.
5.	☿	Raphael.	♃	Sachiel.	♀	Anael.
6.	☽	Gabriel.	♂	Samael.	☿	Raphael.
7.	♄	Cassiel.	☉	Michael.	☽	Gabriel.
8.	♃	Sachiel.	♀	Anael.	♄	Cassiel.
9.	♂	Samael.	☿	Raphael.	♃	Sachiel.
10.	☉	Michael.	☽	Gabriel.	♂	Samael.
11.	♀	Anael.	♄	Cassiel.	☉	Michael.
12.	☿	Raphael.	♃	Sachiel.	♀	Anael.

Hour.	WEDNESDAY. Night.		THURSDAY. Night.		FRIDAY. Night.		SATURDAY. Night.	
1.	☉	Michael.	☽	Gabriel.	♂	Samael.	☿	Raphael.
2.	♀	Anael.	♄	Cassiel.	☉	Michael.	☽	Gabriel.
3.	☿	Raphael.	♃	Sachiel.	♀	Anael.	♄	Cassiel.
4.	☽	Gabriel.	♂	Samael.	☿	Raphael.	♃	Sachiel.
5.	♄	Cassiel.	☉	Michael.	☽	Gabriel.	♂	Samael.
6.	♃	Sachiel.	♀	Anael.	♄	Cassiel.	☉	Michael.
7.	♂	Samael.	☿	Raphael.	♃	Sachiel.	♀	Anael.
8.	☉	Michael.	☽	Gabriel.	♂	Samael.	☿	Raphael.
9.	♀	Anael.	♄	Cassiel.	☉	Michael.	☽	Gabriel.
10.	☿	Raphael.	♃	Sachiel.	♀	Anael.	♄	Cassiel.
11.	☽	Gabriel.	♂	Samael.	☿	Raphael.	♃	Sachiel.
12.	♄	Cassiel.	☉	Michael.	☽	Gabriel.	♂	Samael.

SUMMARY OF PRACTICAL DIRECTIONS FOR MODERN EXPERIMENTERS, OR BEGINNERS.

IT will have been noticed by the reader that the ancient methods of crystal-gazing for purposes of divination involved a somewhat elaborate ritual, including the use of swords, pentacles, candles, and many of the accompaniments usual to the performance of magical rites in bygone ages, when the object in view was not as at present, the cultivation of mere personal clairvoyance in the gazer, but rather to compel the actual presence in the crystal of certain genii or spirits, and to obtain therefrom answers to such questions as might be propounded by the querent.

While, therefore, it has been of interest to trace in the foregoing pages the *historical* aspect of this subject, it will be well for all persons into whose hands this book may fall to remember carefully the two following points :—

(a) That the *modus operandi* pursued by certain of the ancients, and in which the paraphernalia and ritual described were utilised, was one involving dangers of no mean order, as has been already pointed out, and could only be properly made use of by highly qualified votaries who had received personal training under some practical and expert master of the ceremonial, who understood the unseen forces of the spiritual world, both good and

evil, and the necessary steps to be taken for pro-
tecting themselves from possible injury, or even
death, through the medium of wicked intelligences.

(*b*) That as the ordinary experimenter of to-day has no
desire to compel the presence of a spiritual being
in the crystal, it is quite unnecessary for him or
her to draw magic circles, or to go to the trouble
and expense of acquiring and using special or
costly apparatus, with the exception of the crystal
itself.

What *is* desired is through the regular use of
the translucent sphere *to cultivate a personal
degree of clairvoyant power*, so that visions of
things or events, past, present, and future, may
appear clearly to the interior vision, or eye of the
soul.

In the pursuit of this effort only, the crystal becomes at once both a beautiful, interesting, and
harmless channel of pleasure and instruction,
shorn of its former dangers, and rendered conducive to mental development.

To the attainment of this desirable end, attention is asked to the following practical directions,
which, if carefully followed, will lead to success:

(1) Select a quiet room where you will be entirely undisturbed, taking care that it is as far as
possible free from mirrors, ornaments, pictures,
glaring colours, and the like, which may otherwise distract the attention.

The room should be of comfortable tempera-
ture in accordance with the time of year, neither

hot nor cold. About 60° to 65° Fahr. is suitable in most cases, though allowance can be made where necessary for natural differences in the temperaments of various persons. Thus thin, nervous, delicately - organised individuals, and those of lymphatic and soft, easy-going, passive types, require a slightly warmer apartment than the more positive class, who are known by their *dark* eyes, hair, and complexion, combined with more prominent joints and sharper development of what phrenologists term the Perceptive region of the forehead. Should a fire, or any form of artificial light be necessary, it should be well screened off, so as to prevent the light rays from being reflected in, or in any manner directly reaching the crystal.

The room should not be dark, but rather shadowed, or charged with a dull light, somewhat such as prevails on a cloudy or wet day.

(2) The crystal should be placed on its stand on a table, or it may rest on a black velvet cushion, but in either case it should be partially surrounded by a black silk or similar wrap or screen, so adjusted as to cut off any undesirable reflection.

Before beginning to experiment, remember that most frequently nothing will be seen on the first occasion, and possibly not for several sittings, though some sitters, if strongly gifted with psychic powers in a state of unconscious, and sometimes conscious degree of unfoldment, may be fortunate enough to obtain good results at the very first trial.

If, therefore, nothing is perceived during the first few attempts, do not despair or become impatient, or imagine that you will never see anything.

There is a royal road to crystal vision, but it is open only to the compound password of Calmness, Patience, and Perseverance. If at the first attempt to ride a bicycle failure ensues, the only way to learn is to pay attention to the necessary rules, and to *persevere daily* until the ability to ride comes naturally.

Thus it is with the would-be seer. Persevere in accordance with these simple directions, and success will sooner or later crown your efforts.

(3) Commence by sitting comfortably with the eyes fixed upon the crystal, not by a fierce stare, but with a steady, calm gaze, for ten minutes only, on the first occasion. In taking the time it is best to hang your watch at a distance, where, while the face is clearly visible, the ticking is rendered inaudible. When the time is up, carefully put the crystal away in its case, and keep it in a dark place, under lock and key, allowing no one but yourself to handle it.

At the second sitting, which should be *at the same place,** in the same position,* and *at the same time,* you may increase the length of the effort to fifteen minutes, and continue for this period

---

* This precise order of repetition is always to be followed until the experimenter has developed an almost automatic ability to readily obtain results, when it need no longer be adhered to.

during the next five or six sittings, after which
the time may be *gradually* increased, but should
in no case exceed one hour.

(4) Any person or persons admitted to the room,
and allowed to remain while you sit, should (*a*)
keep absolute silence, and (*b*) remain seated at a
distance from you.

When you have developed your latent powers,
questions may, of course, be put to you by one of
those present, but even then only in a very gentle,
or low and slow tone of voice; never suddenly, or
in a forceful manner.

(5) When you find the crystal begins to look dull or
cloudy, with small pin points of light glittering
therein, like tiny stars, you may know that you
are *commencing* to obtain that for which you
seek—viz., crystalline vision. Therefore persevere with confidence. This condition may, or may
not, continue for several sittings, the crystal seeming at times to alternately appear and disappear,
as in a mist. By and by this hazy appearance
will in its turn give place quite suddenly to a
blindness of the senses to all else but a blue or
bluish ocean of space, against which, as if it were
a background, *the vision* will be clearly apparent.

(6) The crystal should not be used soon after taking
a meal, and care should be taken in matters of
diet to partake only of digestible foods, and to
avoid alcoholic beverages. Plain and nourishing
food, and outdoor exercise, with contentment of
mind, or love of simplicity in living, are great aids

to success. Mental anxiety, or ill-health, are not conducive to the desired end. Attention to correct breathing is of importance.

(7) As regards the time at which events seen will come to pass, each seer is usually impressed with regard thereto; but, as a general rule, visions appearing in the extreme background indicate time more remote, either past or future, than those perceived nearer at hand, while those appearing in the forefront, or close to the seer, denote the present, or immediate future.

(8) Two principal classes of visions will present themselves to the sitter—(*a*) The Symbolic, indicated by the appearance of symbols such as a flag, boat, knife, gold, etc.; and (*b*) Actual Scenes and Personages, in action or otherwise.

Persons of a Positive cast of organisation, the more active, excitable, yet decided type, are most likely to perceive symbolically, or allegorically; while those of a Passive nature usually receive direct or literal revelations. Both classes will find it necessary to carefully cultivate truthfulness, unselfishness, gratitude for what is shown, and absolute confidence in the Love, Wisdom, and Guidance of God Himself.

HYGIENIC CLAIRVOYANCE.

HYGIENIC CLAIRVOYANCE.

INTRODUCTION.

THE subject of Hygienic Clairvoyance, however novel it may appear to modern readers, is not new to the world.

The ancient Grecian philosophers, Pythagoras and Plato, and their successors, who discoursed of Hygiene as a department of human wisdom, had recourse to Clairvoyance —the Clear Sight of the Magnetic sleep.

They regarded the clairvoyant, or clear-see-er, as a living entrance-door to the sacred temple of Inner Realities. They knew that to such an one the Internal becomes, without the use of the outer senses, more perceptible than the External is to us by the ordinary mode of objective perception.

Pythagoras received his instruction in this subject in the temples of Egypt, in which, as well as in those of ancient India, there are representations of individuals being put into the magnetic sleep by the same simple process which we moderns have, of late years, discovered to be effective.

The family of Hippocrates, " the Father of Physic," were, it is recorded, ministers in the temple of Æsculapius. Hippocrates' knowledge of Clairvoyance is shown by the following passage — now no longer obscure — in his writings : —" *The sight being closed to the external, the soul perceives truly the affections of the body.*" This exactly states the case of the Clairvoyant. He used to treat some disorders by the application of the hands; in other words, he used to magnetise—or, as we in these days would say, mesmerise—the patient, probably under clairvoyant indications.

Pythagoras himself, Iamblichus states, used this means to procure quiet sleep, with good and prophetic dreams. He even says, probably from analogous knowledge, that the art of Medicine *originated* in this "divine sleep," for Iamblichus speaks of being himself a subject of the magnetic sleep.

Æsculapius is said, according to Cicero, who wrote on this subject, to have uttered oracles in the temple sleep, for the cure of the sick.

If we turn to the sacred Scriptures, we there learn many things in relation to this subject. Moses, it may be inferred, with other lore of the Egyptians, was instructed by their wise men in this magnetic science. We read of a youth being restored to life by a prophet; of an angel indicating the means of Tobias recovering his sight, etc. But the Scriptures being accessible to all, we need not refer further to them.

The Jewish philosophic sect, the Essenes, it is matter of history, also taught the system, and practised it, of healing by "laying on of hands." It may be inferred that they knew also of Hygienic Clairvoyance, which is but an advanced chapter out of the same book.

The Romans, who received their philosophy from Greece, could not but be acquainted with this department of it; and so we read without surprise that, with them as with the Greeks, the sick used to be brought to the temples, where remedies were revealed by this means for their disorders.

Celsus, the great Roman physician, according to Asclepiades, was familiar with the science.   Tacitus records
that in obedience to a vision of the god Serapis, two men—
one blind, and the other lame of an arm—had recourse to
the Emperor Vespasian, at Alexandria, and they were
cured by simple processes which we should call Magnetic.
Suetonius relates the same fact, circumstantially.

Strabo speaks of a certain place on the Asian shore,
consecrated to Pluto and Proserpine, to which the sick
were brought to be prescribed for by the priests during
the magnetic sleep.

The Sibyls—virgin prophetesses of the Temple of Jupiter;
in other phrase, clairvoyantes under care of the priests of
the temple—according to Saint Justin, declared many true
things, and when the intelligence which animated them was
withdrawn, remembered nothing of what they had said.
This describes Clairvoyance.

We might also quote authorities to show that the Druidesses of Britain and Gaul were clairvoyantes, having among
their functions the hygienic one of discriminating and pre-
scribing for disease.

There has been, indeed, no nation, from the earliest times,
without this science.   But the knowledge of it was not
solely in the possession of temples and schools; but wherever deposited, this knowledge could only be expected to be
found in the records of Philosophy.   But when younger and
barbarous nations overran Europe, philosophy was put into
abeyance, and its records passed out of the light of day.
From the darkness consequent upon their incursions slowly
emerged other philosophies, all exhibiting incompleteness,
until at length Europe is practically under the sway of one

which is distinctively styled "Natural," from which the subject on which we are engaged is excluded. Of course this "Natural" philosophy is the opposite of a "Spiritual" philosophy, of which Clairvoyance is an item and exponent. But parallel with the decadence of ancient philosophy and worship, there arose the new Christian religion, and something of that which the former lost was saved by the latter.

The records, therefore, of our subject, which then became wanting in philosophy, are to be looked for in the archives of churches and religious institutions. And thus, as Alphonse Teste remarks, we find this subject in the middle ages intimately blended with that of religion in all the Christian nations.

"The churches," says the historian Mialle, "in this matter succeeded the temples of the ancients, in which were consigned the traditions and the processes of Magnetism. There were the same customs of passing the nights in them, the same dreams, the same visions, the same cures."

The Church in those days recognised practically "the gifts of healing," as among those other gifts of the Spirit (1 Cor. xii. 7-11), of which it held itself to be the sacred custodian. But whatever our subject gained under the sanction of the Church, was associated with religious faith rather than with science. Hence the disfavour in which the records of it, by ecclesiastics, are held by our modern scientific professors. And when philosophy did find its way among churchmen, it was of the one-sided and sceptical kind which prevailed among the laity of the time, and thus with them also the subject fell into discredit. They agreed with the lay philosophers in regarding all such records (to borrow David Hume's words in commenting upon Vespasian's marvellous cures) as the "palpable falsehoods of exploded superstition."

But however ready the general mind to ignore, or deny, the fine truths involved in this subject, there were facts of continual occurrence which could not but attract the attention of independent and original observers, and who, from time to time, endeavoured to claim for them a place in the philosophy of their day.

A century before Mesmer's discovery, Van Helmont wrote:—"Magnetism is in action everywhere; there is nothing new in it but the name; it is a paradox, strange and fantastical, *only to those who are sceptical of everything*, or who attribute to the power of the Devil that which they themselves cannot render account of."

It is to the *resuscitation* of Magnetic science, under the auspices of Mesmer and his school, that the revival of the philosophic study and application of Hygienic Clairvoyance is due. It is this school which furnishes modern testimony, abundant and varied, to the value and importance of our subject. Excellent contributions have been furnished to it of late years by Ennemoser,[1] Mayo, Townshend, Haddock, Davis, Dods, Cahagnet, Dupotet, Teste, and others too numerous to mention, both in Europe and America.

The advocates of Mesmeric science having established for it an acknowledgment of its applicability in numerous disorders, the writers just named, as some of the advanced of that school, seem to have come forward to vindicate in due course, the higher claims of Clairvoyance to scientific and public recognition.

---

[1] See Howitt's Translation.   H. G. Bohn, 1854.

CLAIRVOYANCE: ITS THEORY AND PRACTICE.

1. In the course of curing by Mesmerism, some patients pass into an extraordinary state, which modern physiologists call an "abnormal" one, and which state is variously divided, by careful observers, into certain ascending degrees.

"As the patient advances in these degrees," says one of these observers (Kluge, of Berlin), "so does he seem to recede from the sensuous world."

This state, however, even in its lowest degree, cannot be induced in all patients ; nor is an ascent in it, to the highest, requisite for the recovery of health, for many patients remain only in the lowest degree during the whole of their mesmeric treatment up to their complete cure.   Some become more and more influenced by every succeeding operation, progressively ascending to the highest; others, though few, pass to the highest at once, and continue in it, whenever operated upon, to the end of their cure.

"In the first degree," continues Kluge, "the usual channels of access by which the soul communicates with the external world remain open; external sensation being intact, the subject perceives himself still in the ordinary sphere of things : this I call the—

(1) "WAKING DEGREE.   The next is the degree of

(2) "HALF SLEEP.   In it the eyes are closed, but the other senses are not entirely sealed.

(3) "MAGNETIC SLEEP.   In which the patient is as if stupified ; but while thus standing, as it were, upon the verge of the world of sense, he still retains the recollection of actual, or sensuous life.

(4) "SOMNAMBULISM. (Sleep-walking.) This degree is distinguishable from the preceding by the presence of consciousness.

(5) "SELF-INSPECTION. (Introvision.) In this degree [says Kluge] *the patient obtains a luminous knowledge of the interior state of his body and mind*, diagnoses his complaint, and indicates the most effectual remedies for its cure.

(6) "CLAIRVOYANCE, or GENERAL VISION. In the sixth degree the patient passes the bounds of his own corporeity and enters into *rapport*, or relation, *with objects in universal nature;* the faculty of Introvision becomes exalted into that of EXTROVISION (Clairvoyance), extending to and into objects and individualities, near and remote, in space and time."

2. Thus far I agree with Kluge. He goes on to say that in this degree " the patient becomes abstracted from all things mean and terrestrial, and is exalted to the grandest and noblest sentiment; he undergoes a transmutation of being; a spirit speaks through him, etc." But this extra-elevation above Clairvoyance clearly marks a seventh degree —that of EXTASIS, or TRANCE (from *transitus animae*—the passing of the soul to the other side), that degree in which there is interior relation with the individualities and objects of the spiritual world, and which is largely treated of by other observers.

This, however, merely in passing, for we have nothing to do at present with the subject of *Extasis*—we pause at that of CLAIRVOYANCE, that degree of the state in which the subject transcends the bounds of his own corporeity, and is able to enter into immediate *rapport* with external objects and individuals of this world.

With this definition of the faculty of CLAIRVOYANCE it will next be for us to consider some instances of it in exercise.

3. Before doing this let us dwell a little upon the cry that the faculty in question is " abnormal," " morbid," more especially in cases where it occurs *spontaneously*, of the frequency of which we have abundant instances.

4. The physiologist, *par excellence*, will systematise and ratiocinate from night till morn, and from morn till night again, upon the perceptions and experience of his own five senses—nay, to strain a point, he will sometimes argue his possession of a sixth; but beyond that—nothing! But man possesses not only the faculties of *external* perception and reason, but those of *internal* perception, of intuition and instinct of a higher degree, corresponding to the intuition and instinct of all animated beings, and which are as serviceable to the species as is his observation of things by the external senses.

Under the actuation of instinct, animals move from place to place, from region to region, and distinguish wholesome from noxious plants. By the same faculties in man, did he not, in the early times of the race, discover the qualities of many of our traditional medicines ? In those early times those interior faculties seem to have been more active than that of reason; while in the times approaching our own, the faculty of reason has borne sway, and been more fostered.

Nevertheless, the intuitive and instinctive faculties, being as innate in man as in all animals, have ever been stronger or weaker, more or less active, guides of the race ; but not being recognised by the *esprit philosophe*, the records of their activity appear only sparsely and obscurely in the

annals of European civilisation—the culminating character-
istic of which has been the cultivation of the sensuous and
the rational.

5. The "solid" school, which has arisen out of this cultivation, furnishes us with those who have been designated
the *materialists* in medicine.

When such an one is called to a subject in any of the
degrees of this extraordinary state, occurring spontaneously,
he forthwith finds a name in his nosology with which to
label it; tells people that the phenomena which strike them
as singular are nothing more than the symptoms of a
"certain morbid condition" of the nervous system; and if
his audience can appreciate him, he may talk about the
"great sympathetic," and "reflex action," and "spine," and
"brain," and, with a final "hope to set all right," makes a
rush at his bottles.

6. For the comfort of this class of patients, however, it
should be said that, since the days of Mesmer and Hahnemann, there has been a gradual decrease in unanimity as to
this "rush at the bottles."

But as there are materialist-homœopathists, so there are
(*mirabile dictu*), materialist-mesmerists; the former going
to work against the "zoo-magnetic state," with his dynamised phosphorus perhaps; the latter with his "curative"
passes and mesmerised water. With both of these, notwithstanding their higher methods, the extraordinary state is a
morbid one to be cured. And so I leave them, for the
present, to settle between themselves which of their processes
is the better.

7. Psychologists, with Kluge, infer from all its phenomena
that *Clairvoyance* is a faculty *common to humanity,* but

exercised by the being when in a certain state, which occurs *spontaneously*, but which may be *induced* by various agencies and means; that in this state the soul which perceives is more or less freed from its body; that the state is therefore a psychical or spiritual state. That this is but a rational inference, will be evident to all who fearlessly contemplate the phenomena with the straightforward look of truth-seekers, rather than with the oblique glance of those who love best their own foregone conclusions.

8. Within the last few years the records of this faculty of *Clairvoyance*, spontaneous and induced, have been numerous.

Although it is denied that *Clairvoyance* is a symptom of disorder, inasmuch as it presents itself in normal health, yet it is readily granted that it frequently presents itself where the subjects, always of the Nervous Temperament, have suffered from illness; though, even then, such illness may be an *effect* of a changing state from within, of the Nervous System; and more particularly if the patient has been subjected to the action of opium, *cannabis sativa*, ethers, magnetism, etc., all of which augment its sensibility.

But indeed clairvoyance presents itself in subjects in all states of health: verified instances of this are abundant enough to fill volumes.

It is painful sometimes to contemplate the straining of some of our " philosophers " in their efforts to debase every mental manifestation, above sensuous perception, into a symptom of organic disorder. With such " philosophers " genius would stand as delirium, poetry as insanity, inspiration as illusion, bringing their subjects properly under the treatment of the doctor and druggist.

Clairvoyance is truly a department of the same high and

interior function of the being as these, and to consign it to the correction of the pills of the old school, or trituration of the new, is about as rational as would have been the application of correctives to Pope's physical deformity, *because* he wrote the "*Essay on Man*;" or to the blind bard's eyes *because* he wrote "Paradise Lost;" or as would have been the surreptitious mixing by Swedenborg's house-keeper of physic in her master's coffee, *because* he spoke of things unseen by mortal eye. Clairvoyance the symptom of bodily disorder! Look at the robust Didier, in whom the faculty was in continuous exercise for years. But the faculty, like other faculties, may be *too continuously* exercised. Look at other Clairvoyants, in whom organic health has been almost undisturbed since they have regularly exercised this faculty, and it must be agreed that there is no connection necessarily between the questions of Clairvoyance and Health. Indeed, ill-health operates against the exercise of the faculty in those in whom it is developed. The Clairvoyante of the greatest lucidity I have ever known, in questions connected with health, on one occasion, when her health had received a shock from some sudden excitement, was not able to pass into the state even of *Introvision* until she was convalescent; nor could she resume her *clairvoyant* examinations until she had regained her ordinary good health.

The psychological or spiritual school holds that every being and naturally formed object is, in its beginning, a spiritual or monadial entity; that having its *origin in*, it must necessarily have *continuous relations with, the spiritual* or monadial plane of existence, *as well as with the material* or sensuous plane in which it is made to develop itself; that each, according to species, etc., evolves from its monadial centre an essential *aura*, which has positive and negative magnetoid relations with the essential aura of every other.

Mesmeric attraction and repulsion exhibit a strong analogy with magnetic attraction and repulsion. Analogous attraction and repulsion obtains not only between individuals of the same but of different species, not only in animate, but in inanimate nature.

ILLUSTRATIONS AND CASES OF CLAIRVOYANCE.

The facts here brought forward lead the mind rationally to the conclusions arrived at by Mesmer and Hahnemann—conclusions harmonious with those of earlier philosophers, however variously expressed in terms, namely, that all the beings and objects of Nature act and react dynamically (monadially or spiritually) upon each other; that it is the *spirit* which *dynamically acts* and *reacts* in the body; that the *action of medicines* is *dynamical* upon the *spirit* of the patient.

On July 2, 18—, I invited a few friends to be present during the investigation by a clairvoyante (Mrs. W.), through the *natural faculty* possessed by her in an eminent degree of *dynamically* perceiving and distinguishing objects. It had been proposed to magnetise her, but she said it was not necessary to be in the sleep to exercise her dynamic faculty: by collecting herself, and *willing*, she could perceive the qualities and magnetoid relations of objects. Our preparations and arrangements having been made beforehand the clairvoyante was invited into the room. She entered, and approached the table, on which were placed under separate papers, a few inches apart, the following substances :—Bismuth, silver, gold, copper. I had made some transverse passes over each to remove all foreign effluences from them. Putting her hand upon the paper covering the bismuth, she said, "This feels something like zinc, but I am not sure." Leaving that, she moved her hand over the paper covering the silver; she said, "Silver is there; it burns, because it is so near to this, which must be gold." Her mistaking the bismuth for zinc, she said, was its being too near to the copper. On bringing her hand over the paper concealing the copper it became cramped and distorted. To relieve this I made transverse passes over the hand and arm, but in vain. "De-magnetise the copper," she said. I made transverse passes over the copper, and the cramp of the hand ceased after a few moments. It must be remembered I had made passes over the copper at the commencement. She said that the metals had all been placed too near each other; that *any two metals*, she had found, made a battery: the positive with the metals negative to them. She remarked incidentally that the sun's rays were the most effective in restoring the proper magnetism to metals; and that according to her observations all medicines make batteries with each other—in other words, have positive and negative dynamical relations. Her faculty not appearing to be sufficiently free from external influence, it was proposed she should be put into "the sleep." For this purpose, on the present occasion, she selected my magnetism, as it was about her since my attempt to free her indirectly from the effluence of the copper.

But before magnetising her she wished me to remove my chain, as the effluence from that might affect her; the *copper* she said had made her feel *combative*. She passed "behind the veil," as I might term it, after being magnetised by the eye for something less than a minute.

As soon as she intimated, by her usual gesture, that she was in "the other state," I proposed that the friends present should place themselves *en rapport* with her, as usual, by touching her hand.

"No," she said; "I see and hear you well enough."

This was unusual, and the reason was not asked; perhaps it lay in the fact of all present being friendly with her, and earnest inquirers into the subject.

She then at once reached her hand to a lady—an invalid recovering from a paralytic affection—and said, "In extreme cases of paralysis a battery like one of these might be worn on the arm, and one of copper and zinc on the thigh, for the battery on the arm will not affect the legs." (Her hand here accidentally touched the *brass* moulding, lined with lead, on the arm of the chair she was in; she shook her hand, blew on it, and said, "Nasty.") "There should be a change from time to time; the zinc should sometimes be in contact with the skin, and at other times the copper; the *zinc* should *touch the copper* at the *edges*, but *not* in the *centre*. These directions are for a *hard, dark person;* if *fair, reverse* the order. In many cases of the loss of the use of the leg and arm, the paralysis is from congestion in the tissues of the brain; in such cases the best battery would be a *film of platina* on a *zinc foundation*, with thin paper interposed. Lead and brass make a good battery for some cases also. Mrs. B. (one of the ladies present) should have a *thin sheet* of *brass* to her *feet*, and *thin lead* to the nape of her *neck*, and the places to which the metals are applied should be washed at times with *camphor water*. She would be better in a fortnight."

The Clairvoyante was at this stage awakened by a few reverse passes. While she rested, Mr. B. and the friends present were comparing notes as to the process by which the Mind took cognisance and dynamically valued objects. One said that the mind seemed to him to have the power of polarising itself to objects, and of receiving impressions from them, and more, which I do not remember. In the meantime Mrs. W. (the Clairvoyante), who had appeared to be listening to the conversation, had passed unobserved into "the sleep," and broke in with, "Pardon me, the whole operation is spiritual; from the time of your willing to magnetise the subject to sleep, the vital electricity of the operator is only made use of as a medium for a spirit to convey his own magnetism to operate upon him or her, and whom you then call clairvoyant. A spirit, or spirits, hover over and conduct the operations, and bring the spirit of the subject into relation with that of the things under examination." I simply state this here, and the words must be taken for what they may appear to be worth.

I said, " You told us just now that spirits take part in these inquiries, may I ask who are now favouring us ? " She replied at once, " Dr. Ley and Sir Charles Bell."

I thought this very singular.

Dr. Hugh Ley, of Middlesex Hospital, was physician to the Charlotte Street Dispensary, to the surgeon of which, Mr. Hugh Carolan, I was articled in 1821 ; and I had, six

years subsequently, attended the practice of Sir Charles at
Middlesex Hospital—particulars quite unknown to Mrs. W.
in her ordinary state.

" Do they remember me ? "

" Dr. Ley says he remembers you from a boy ; Sir Charles
is reminded of you by Dr. Ley ; he did not remember you
at first."

I took the words of the clairvoyante for what they
appeared to be worth. I said I was happy to be thus
remembered, and would take the opportunity of asking
their present view of the *modus operandi* of medicines, as
they used to administer them.

The answer was at once given :—

" As a battery with the mucous tissue of the stomach, the
excitant being the acid or alkali in the stomach."

Mrs. W. having been in " the sleep " the prescribed time,
she was restored to the ordinary state.

At our next sitting, Mrs. W. being put to sleep in the
usual manner by her husband (who attended to conduct the
experiments), four metals, in separate boxes, were placed on
the table. She took up one box, and said, " Silver is here ;
it makes my mouth fill with water."

" De-magnetise the metal, and give me the antimony ; it
antidotes the silver."

Presently she threw these aside, and reached another of
the boxes ; opened it, took out the metal, and put it into
her mouth.

She said, " This metal (it was NICKEL) is very good for
fits. It should be prepared by trituration. But the patient
should be carefully watched while taking it, for it will
produce salivation : it will *antidote Mercury*. It is good

for Epileptic Fits, whether produced by the irritation of worms or otherwise."

She then gave directions as to the dose, with respect to age and sex. The exactness of the mode of preparing it for medicinal use was singular, and would do credit to the very "spirit" of Hahnemann, about whom she knew absolutely nothing. It is, omitting repetitions, as follows, word for word :—

"Take six grains of the nickel, and having treated it in the usual way for triturating metal, digest it in a little alcohol for one hour ; then triturate again for an hour all one way, thus (moving the hand, holding an ideal pestle, from left to right circularly) ; then shake for an hour with ten ounces of alcohol. All this to be done by one person : he should cover the cork with his right hand, and at every succussion bring down the bottom of the bottle into the left palm. One drop of this tincture would be an average dose.

"An overdose of it would be antidoted with homœopathic (dynamised) mercury.

"There is not one case in ten where fits would not be removed by one or two drops every hour with a teaspoonful of water, abating as the symptoms diminished.

"Bah ! it tastes bad. Give me the silver ; *silver antidotes nickel* as well as *mercury*.

"When nickel, in some rare cases, does not cure, mesmerism will, if care is had to the relative temperament of the mesmeriser and patient. When I go away, I shall call at the *fishmonger's* up here, and put an *oyster, without the beard,* in my mouth, and hold it there for a minute ; it will receive the effect of these metals."

"What will you do with it then ?"

"You don't suppose I shall swallow it?"

Here I awakened her.

The regularity of our sittings was interrupted by engage-
ments on one side or the other.

At our next, however (August 5th), on being put "to
sleep" with the same metals before her, she took the *nickel*
and said, "I told you *nickel* was good for *fits*, but it will
also produce *inflammation* of the *throat* and *eyes*. If you
were to give it *after mercury* you would produce a battery
which would excite the *carotids*; to *counteract* which effect
arsenicum would be required, in *sensible*, not infinitesimal
doses. It would produce *inflammation* of the *surface* of the
lungs, of the appearance of erysipelas: the *symptoms* for
administering it curatively would be *sensations of heat and*
tingling. The *tincture of nickel* should be given, *three*
doses of it. The patient should be, as it were, salivated.

"I have told you how to prepare a tincture, but I see that
you might give in EPILEPSY large doses of the third trituration of it. In *bad cases* a dose *every two hours*, until a
sensible effect appeared; then lengthen the intervals until a
decided change is produced. Then give the *mercurius*
twice a-day for two days; afterwards *hepar sulphuris*."

The same sitting she went through a similar examination
of *bismuth*, and particularised its therapeutic uses.

August 31st.—After being put "to sleep" she said,
"When you put me to sleep for metals don't stand so near
me as when for other things."

"Very well. What will you look at this evening?"

"Manganese."

The manganese was handed to her, and the other metals
were removed.

"Doctor, this sends the blood up to the head. It is good for insane patients. And it produces congestion and torpor of the venous system."

At this moment my son came hastily in with a message to me; he said, "That second dose of oil has not acted, and they want to know what to do."

The clairvoyante turned sharply round and said, "Give an enema, to be sure."

I said, "Ah, perhaps you will leave the manganese, and look at the case?"

"Yes." (After a pause)—"I am ready. Touch Robert's hand; he is fresh from the patient."

She did so. "Oh, it's your little niece."

"Yes; what is the matter with her?"

"It is bad indigestion; she's swallowed a plum-stone."

"Do you perceive it?"

"Yes; it is in what I call the second stomach—what you call the *duodenum*. That is in an irritable state: and as it contracts upon the plum-stone, it is thrown into pain and spasm. It is going into inflammation."

"What should be done?"

"Give now an enema of warm water, and place the patient in a hot bath. Afterwards administer aconite."

"Thank you. Will you leave the child now and come back to the manganese?"

"Yes, we'll take her back to the Hampstead Road—there, that's right."

"Now then for the manganese."

With respect to this incident, it is to be remarked that Mrs W. knew nothing, in her ordinary state, of this little niece, nor any of the particulars which she clearly perceived.

I had been called to my little niece in the morning of the
same day, and found her suffering colicky pains, and
suspecting the presence of some foreign body in the intes-
tines, though not of a plum-stone, I directed a dose of castor
oil to be given ; to be repeated if required.   On enquiry
next day, there appeared good reason to believe that the
clairvoyante perceived truly in this case.

With respect to the clairvoyante " taking back " the child
in idea, it is to be remarked that she generally expressed
herself in the same way with respect to children whom she
had examined at a distance.   I imagine it to mean, that in
detaching her own *rapport* with the child, she sees that the
mother's *rapport* is intact.

She resumed her discourse about the manganese thus :—

" If you are called to a patient who has been *drinking
excessively*, give him, if a strong man, one drop of the first
dilution every two hours, until better ; then lengthen the
intervals to six hours ; then lessen the dose.   While giving
manganese, keep the bowels in action with the first trituration of sulphur.   This manganese makes me feel very lazy ;
we'll leave it now, please."

Here we will now take leave of the metals for the
present.

I remarked at the outset that it is not for me to discuss
here the question of *Extasis;* nevertheless a few words at
this point may not be amiss, with respect to what the
clairvoyante said about the *intervention of spirits* in the
phenomena under examination.

In the first place, let us keep in mind that we, in the
material or earthly body, are as really spirits as those who
have vacated this mortal frame.

Secondly, that *Clairvoyance* is thus a *faculty*, exercised by a human *spirit clothed in a body*.

Thirdly, that the *body* of the subject should ever be *in health* for the exercise of the lucid faculty.

Fourthly, that, as is well known, the faculty in any individual is, like other faculties, strengthened by the *regular* and *reasonable* exercise of it.

Fifthly, that the faculty is of a prominently *hereditary* character in some families.

Keeping these several points in mind, we cannot help recognising in Clairvoyance an undoubted exercise of the *individual's own faculty* and powers of perception— *spiritual,* and *at the same time natural.* Of this exercise, we find more or less perfect examples in proportion to the more or less complete magnetoid detachment from the sensuous plane ; the most complete resulting in an inversion of the psychical polarity of the subject, evidenced by the remarkable fact of *the spirit transferring impressions from outer objects to the body* in opposition to the *ordinary course* of *the body conveying them to the spirit.*

Mrs. W. was on one occasion the means of saving human life under the following circumstances :—

Mr. John Tilbury, coachbuilder, of the New Road, was a neighbour of Mrs. W., and used to bring in friends to put her clairvoyance to the test. One day, in making a casual call, in conversation he remarked he had somehow injured his watch. While he was there Mrs. W. was put to sleep, and she, without suggestion, referred to his watch, and asked him what he expected *if he was so foolish as to pick the works with a pin ?*

" Do you mean to say that you see that I have done so ? "

" Yes."

" If you really see the interior of the watch what is its number ? "

She gave the number, consisting of half the figures of the numeration table.   On comparison it was found correct. Mr. Tilbury expressed his astonishment.

" I am able to tell you something better worth knowing than that," said the clairvoyante.   " I see something that is likely to happen to your son Charles ; he is likely to be bitten by a dog, and if he is, he'll die."

" What dog ? "

" He's a mischievous boy, and he'll poke the dog with a stick, and I see the stick he is likely to use ; it is a hooked one ; it is in a stack of timber in a shed in your yard."

" But what dog I ask ?   I have no dog."

" Oh, the dog will be sent to you—he is a spotted dog : he will come in a basket. in a dog-cart from Pinner ; a friend will send him to you.   If he comes, the boy will be likely to worry him with the stick, and if so it will lead to the boy's death."

Now, Mr. Tilbury expected no dog ; but on his return home found a letter awaiting him, informing him that a dog would be sent by a sporting friend of his, living at Pinner, for him to take care of.   He also found the hooked stick as pointed out by the clairvoyante, and his son claimed it as his play-stick.   He saw the possibility and probability of mischief accruing if Master Charlie and the dog came together, and, like a reasonable man, deliberated with his wife, who immediately posted to Pinner.   Mrs. Tilbury on her arrival there, found that a dog was actually about to be despatched ; that he was a spotted, high-bred pointer, fierce, and very likely to bite if poked with a stick ; that he was about to be put in a basket to be forwarded by a dog-cart.

In this case the clairvoyante perceived the cause of an impending evil, *and thus enabled the boy's parents to avert it.* This is a valuable instance of the exercise of the clairvoyant faculty.

Ancient philosophy recognised a *reciprocal influence among all entities ;* between the Earth and all the naturally-formed things and beings on it, and between these and the sun, moon, planets, stars—the visible bodies of the macrocosm. It also included among entities, *invisible or spiritual beings,* under various names, to whom it accorded a greater or lesser influence among the entities of the Earth. The foundations of this philosophy were laid by seers, prophets, oracles—those who were pre-eminently subject of the "divine sleep," the trance. Upon the breaking up of ancient civilisation the philosophy disappeared, except so much as was, in its spiritual part, purified in the Christian religion, and as it was, in its scientific part, fragmentarily caught up by students of natural philosophy, of whom we have examples in the greater or lesser lights of the so-called "dark ages," and—approaching more modern days—in Paracelsus, Van Helmont, Friar Bacon, and many others.

In the early Christian Church the influence and action of spiritual beings, for the purposes of health (as, for instance, in the Bible story of the troubling of the waters of a certain pool by an angelic being), were as much acknowledged by worshippers as in the temples of their ancestors. This acknowledgment is *still made* by some sects of the Church,

and doubtless whatever individual opinion may be held
regarding the general tenets of Roman Catholicism, its
recognition of spiritual or angelic ministrations, represents
the truth concerning this matter.   But when literary
Europe accepted the canons of criticism laid down by
Hume and Voltaire, all this was gradually and erroneously
set down as *bygone superstition,* and it was held that
everything not sensuously present was—in all future time
—to be treated as *non-existent.* A greater delusion was
never promulgated ; yet such was the effect of this material-
istic teaching that men have, even to the present time,
deliberately closed their eyes against the truth, and at the
end of the nineteenth century are still floundering in the
" darkness" which they have fondly attributed to the past.
Even the Medical profession have for many years flouted
and opposed the truths of Mesmerism, to such an extent
indeed that even men of their own colleges—such, for
instance, as the famous Dr. John Elliotson, M.A., L.R.C.P., etc.,
who was in recent years hounded to death in London for his
noble and daring advocacy of PHRENOLOGY and MESMERISM.
Only now is the truth once more dawning, and under the
name of HYPNOTISM a force long opposed is being gradually
accepted and *applied* by such men as Professor Charcot,
Dr. Lloyd Tuckey, and others.

Literature and criticism were in the before-mentioned
condition when Mesmer, upon whom the mantle of Van
Helmont had indirectly fallen, *revived a part of the old
philosophy, viz.,* the reciprocal influence of all visible entities. He demonstrated that a correspondent property to
that of *polarity* and *inclination* in the *loadstone* was
possessed by *man* and other beings. To this *magnetism*

he applied the name of " ANIMAL "—to *distinguish* it in use from the MINERAL kind.   Tracing *disturbance of health* in many cases to *disturbance of Magnetic polarity,* he and his followers showed that by *restoring polarity* health might be frequently restored.   Patients treated by magnetism sometimes pass into a new state.   This state was found to be divisible into various degrees.

In the *ultimate degrees* of this state the patient passes the bounds of corporeity and enters into *rapport* with other objects and individualities, near and remote in space and time—these are CLAIRVOYANCE and TRANCE.   The *nerve-organism* of the human being taken as a whole is *bi-polar*—the *Brain-system* representing *one pole,* the *Ganglionic-system* the *other* ; the two systems being interlaced by reciprocating *nerve-chords* and *nerve-plexuses* into *one system.*   In our ordinary *day-life* the *Brain-system* is *positive,* and the *Ganglionic negative.*   In our ordinary *night-life* the *Ganglionic-system* is *positive,* and the *Brain-system* is *negative*

The *Brain-system* is the focal apparatus of *Sensation* and *Will.*   The *Ganglionic* that of *Intuition, Instinct,* and *Sympathy.*   Facts demonstrate that these apparatuses are the immediate concrete *instruments of the Soul,* by which it has polar organic relations with the material sphere, and thus on the natural plane is made to move spiritual man, who—through the soul—has polar relations also with the spiritual sphere, as manifested in the phenomena of *Clairvoyance* and *Trance.*   In clairvoyance, and in trance especially, we witness a passing from activity on the *external plane* of conscious being to that on an *internal ;* in other words, the essential being is *polarised from* the *natural* to the

spiritual plane; the vito-magnetic currents ceasing, more
or less, to circulate through the *external* nerves, *few
impressions*, or none, are transmitted from *without* to the
brain, but to the organic seat of INSTINCT and INTUITION.
In most subjects the PERCEPTIVE POWERS, are intensified,
and there is, with clear sight of mundane individualities,
spiritual clairvoyance and perhaps clairaudience.   The
degree of change thus effected by this spiritual polarisation
is determined by the idiosyncrasy of the subject; but that,
with the will of the operator, and circumstantial conditions,
has also to be taken into account.

Under some operators subjects will exhibit only the
phenomena of MUNDANE CLAIRVOYANCE, while under others
they will seem to exhibit the *illumination* of *ancient seership.*   This change in the direction of the vito-magnetic
forces of the soul, may be induced in sensitive subjects, *not
only* by the *magnetic process*, but also by the day's
exhaustion of sensibility, irritability, and will; by *various
drugs,* or by wish or passivity, reciprocating, consciously
or unconsciously, with the action of another, visible or
invisible.

For the purpose of explaining hidden states or causes of
disorders, and of searching for hitherto unknown remedies
in nature, the induction of the state by Mesmerism is usual,
and perhaps best.   Clairvoyants, who perceive not only
remote objects on the spiritual plane, may be expected to
be affected by the moral states of persons, and also by the
essential qualities of naturally-formed things.

Every object of the external world—as ancient philosophers taught—whether earth or metal, vegetable or animal,
including the human, has its monadial or soul-substance

perceptible to a correspondent faculty of the human being, when in the state under review. These monadial or soul-substances—otherwise called by various authors, " *vital*," " *sympathial*," " *aural*," " *aromal*," " *essential* " — have magnetic or polar relations with every other, constituting the basis of sympathy or antipathy. Clairvoyants perceive the vapours, rays, or lines of some concordantly intersecting or blending with each other, while they perceive others, on the contrary, constantly repelling.

They perceive further that *each organ of the body* has its *proper magnetism*, and that in the infinitude of natural things there are those who have a magnetism in correspondence with the magnetism of one or other organ. Human magnetism *blends* with that of *water*, producing a resultant of definite activity. Its blending with that of simple drugs explains the activity of the preparations used in Homœopathy, inert except where there is polar reactivity to their action.

The human being—the ultimate of Nature, the microcosm, the universe in small—has, we learn, combined in him the elements of the macrocosm—the universe ; all monadial qualities and forces, all loves and wills—chemical, vegetable, animal—are in him epitomised ; he has thus, in his physical organism, *rapport* or relation with every being and object in visible nature, and, in the constitution of his soul, with beings and objects of the invisible world, even, as we are also divinely assured, unto the Father and Author of All.

Clairvoyants inform us it is the *aura* of a drug, and not its atoms, that constitutes the virtue of the high dilutions, and state that with *this aura* the *preparer's* magnetic fluid *blends*.

In selecting the proper medicine, or its dose, the clairvoyante, sensitive usually with one hand, touches the patient's,
while with the other she touches the phials which have
been chosen and placed before her, to the proper one of
which it is attracted, often strongly; she then seems
mentally to balance or measure the medicine against the
patient. Sometimes she will say there is a *better medicine*
for the case, but does not know the name. Other medicines
being submitted, they are selected in the same manner.
Having once been *en rapport* with a patient in person, a
small lock of hair, new blotting paper on which the patient
has breathed, a glove, or any article which has been in
contact with the subject, will afterwards suffice to reinduce
the original connection between the Seer and his subject.

SUMMARY.

In the course of my observations, I have noticed incidentally the fact that clairvoyance, so interesting in all
its phases to psychologists, is sometimes induced, as well
as clairaudience, by spiritual operation. The subjects of
this kind of Clairvoyance are *ecstatics*, properly so called.
This department, as spiritual clairvoyance, properly forms
the topic for divines to write about rather than physicians.
Clairvoyance is sometimes remotely induced by the operation of natural objects. Kœner, Reichenbach, Ashburner—
his annotator—and others, have demonstrated that some
subjects have their normal polarity disturbed, more or less
completely inverted, by the action of natural objects upon
them. This department, as natural clairvoyance, properly

belongs to natural philosophers, and we shall hail the day when they recognise it as being in their domain.

Clairvoyance, embraced by physical science, and properly induced by medical art by various means, but chief of all by human magnetism, is the department which, as Hygienic Clairvoyance, falls naturally within the province of the physician. This faculty, enabling the perceiving soul to come, while still in the body, into *rapport* with the inner forms, qualities, and states of other beings, and temporal things, enables the physician to investigate all natural objects for hygienic purposes.

In saying this nothing hypothetical or doubtful is declared. The faculty, employed from the earliest ages, has been used for years past by very many of note, for the intuitive perception of diseases, remedies, and antidotes; in the discerning of which, the subject in the clairvoyant state is monadially or spiritually affected by the monadial or spiritual properties of the objects under examination.

The distinctive *advantages* presented by the employment of hygienic clairvoyance, to the patient and the physician, are—

1st. Exactness of diagnosis in exploring the seat of any internal disorder, and in obviating the employment of the doubtful stethoscope, the objectionable speculum, etc.

2nd. The exact discrimination of Temperament and Constitutional peculiarity, and correspondingly exact adaptation of medicine and dose.

3rd. Exact appreciation of the Moral state and its condition as cause or consequence of the physical disorder.

4th. The subjective symptoms—those felt only by the
      patient—becoming objective to the physician
      through the clairvoyant's perception.

These are advantages which cannot but be appreciated; and
not more by the patient than by the honest physician.
For how often is he not obliged to confess that ordinary
discrimination is at fault? We all know that the most
acute physicians err sometimes in their diagnosis, even
when aided by the best contrivances invented by ingen-
uity; and where there is error in diagnosis there is
necessarily error in treatment.

How often do we meet with cases where, from inevitable
error of diagnosis, a system of mere *palliation* has been
prescribed on the ground of impossibility of cure.

Such are the cases against which, under Divine Providence,
the physician can successfully cope by the light and aid of
Hygienic Clairvoyance.

MAGNETIC CLAIRVOYANCE

may be induced by holding the head close to the open horns
of a *large* and *powerful* horse-shoe magnet. It may be
suspended from the ceiling, and held to the head lying
down, so that when let go it will spring away, or come in
contact with its armature, so as to close the circuit. A
quartz crystal is almost as good as a horse-shoe magnet for
the foregoing purpose.

All Clairvoyants should, to be useful, successful, and
enduring, cultivate the *habit* of DEEP BREATHING, for all
Brain-power depends largely upon *Lung-power.* Continued
ability cannot exist if deep breathing is neglected.

All Clairvoyants should *feed* on the best things obtainable.

Clairvoyants must exercise great caution in matters relative to the procreative functions. Abstinence in this direction is good, and Total Abstinence is still better. An error in this direction is *fatal to clear vision*, and *may* cause a lengthened *suspension* of power.

Rapid breathing, forcibly, for 90 seconds, while lying down, in connection with the horse-shoe magnet operation, will prove successful in enabling you to see without eyes, if you are a good subject.

All magnetic, odyllic, and mesmeric processes are twenty times more productive of successful results if conducted in—

(1) A *dark room.*

(2) *Next* to a *perfectly dark room*, moonlight or starlight is preferable.

A SUCCESSFUL METHOD OF INDUCING CLAIRVOYANCE.

1. Room partly darkened.
2. Mirror in the *North* end.
3. Subject sits with *back* turned *towards the mirror.*
4. *Operator (Magnetiser), Subject,* and *Mirror* should form a *triangle.*
5. The *subject* sits so that the reflected ray of light (magnetism), from the operator's eye, will strike the back of his or her head—the subject receiving the *reflected ray.*
6. The *subject* is to be *seated* in a chair having all its legs *fully insulated,* and having his or her feet resting on an insulated stool.

7. No part of the subject's dress, or of the chair must touch the floor.

8. *Not a soul* must be in the *North end* of the room.

9. Any other person present must remain quietly seated in the *South, East,* or *West* portion of the room.

10. No *silk* (not even a cravat or ribbon) must be present in the room.

11. *One* soft and gentle *chord* may be played on the piano, but no other on the same evening.

12. Previous to the experiment, two Magnets should be suspended—*One* with the *North Pole up, the other* with the *North Pole down,* so as to embrace the subject's head without much pressure.

13. When the subject is seated, and the Magnets are arranged as before stated, so that the poles antagonise, BE CAREFUL.

14. The *Operator* now takes a prepared bar-magnet in his hand, and *fixing his gaze steadily* on that point of the looking-glass from whence the reflected ray will glance off and strike the *back* of the *Subject's Head,* just between the fork of the northern magnet, he points the bar-magnet directly towards the open *neck* of the Subject. In a few minutes there should be absolute magnetic slumber induced in the Subject, who will then frequently exhibit the most remarkable powers of Clairvoyance.

IN SEEKING TO BECOME CLAIRVOYANT.

Food.—Daily diet should be very light. Fruit, Tea, Coffee, Milk, may be freely used, but *no* Chocolate, Fat, Oysters, or Pastry, and very little Sugar.

Fasting.—Strict fasting for at least twenty-four hours before using the Crystal is advantageous to the success of the experimenter.

Linen must be often changed.

Skin, Head, and Hair must be kept scrupulously clean. The *bath* is the very best preparation for experiments, and no one can reach good results unless perfectly and absolutely clean.

Patience is a most necessary qualification.

Silence.—Perfect stillness should be observed when using the Crystal.

Time.—Usually allow ten to fifteen minutes for *attaining* a Crystal vision. In some cases one or two hours have been known to elapse before any result was obtained.

What is the *difference* between—

(a) Clairvoyance;
(b) Psychometry;
(c) Intuition?

ANSWER.—The first *Sees*, more or less distinctly.
The second *Feels*, with greater or less intensity.
The third *Knows*—*leaps* at results at a single bound.

Clairvoyance depends upon a peculiar condition of the Brain and Nerves. It is compatible with the most robust health, though sometimes the accompaniment of disordered nerves.

There are three principal matters with which it is necessary to make ourselves acquainted, *viz.* :—

> (*a*) The exact method *how,*
> (*b*) The precise spot *where,*
> (*c*) The proper time *when,*

to apply the specific mesmeric current to any particular individual, in order to produce lucidity, or the mesmeric sleep.

WHAT PROPORTIONS OF PERSONS CAN BECOME CLAIRVOYANT?

As a broad rule 75 out of 100 can become *partly lucid.*

63 in 100 can become Sensitives.
45 „ can reach the 2nd degree of Clairvoyance.
32 „ can reach the 3rd   „   „
14 „ can reach the 4th   „   „
5 „ can reach the 5th   „   „
2 „ can reach the 6th   „   „
    Of 100 men, 56 can become Seers.
    Of 200 women, 180 can become Seeresses.

KINDS OF CLAIRVOYANCE.

There are various *kinds* as well as *degrees* of Clairvoyance:—Natural; Medical; Social; Intellectual; Practical; Purely Mental; Ethereal and Divine; General; Special (as in Religion, Philosophy, Science, Art, Education, Love, etc.); Introspection (past); Inspection (present); Projection (future); Mind-Reading.

All *true Genius* is more or less *Clairvoyant,* but of course it does not necessarily follow that all Clairvoyants are geniuses.

GLOSSARY.

Abeyance—Expectant, awaiting.
Abnormal—Unusual.
Abstracted—Absent, inattentive, separated.
Accruing—Arising; increasing.
Aconite—Common monkshood.
Æsculapius—The ancient "Father of Medicine."
Alkali—Anti-acid.
Alphonse Teste—French writer on Mesmerism.
Analogy—Similarity; likeness.
Annals—Records.
Annotator—A writer of notes, or comments.
Antidotes—Internal remedy, anti-poison.
Antipathy—Dislike; antagonism.
Armature—The "keeper" of a magnet.
Arsenicum—Arsenic.
Arterial—Pertaining to the largest blood vessels which carry the scarlet
    blood.
Asclepiades—A celebrated physician of Bithynia.
Ashburner (John)—A London medical man and writer.
Aubrey—An author of the 17th century.
Aura—Emanation from the body, and surrounding it like an atmosphere.
Auspices—Omens; protection or influence.
Avert—To prevent.
Bi-polar—Having two poles.
Bismuth—A brittle brilliant reddish-white mineral.
Canons—Rules or laws.
Carotids—Great arteries of the head or neck.
"Centre"—A nervous localised spot or "organ" in the brain.
Circuit—A circular course.
Clairaudience—Exalted power of hearing
Cognisance—Knowledge.
Colicky—Acute, griping, abdominal pain.
Compatible—Agreeable.
Conception—Imagination; comprehension; holding within the mind.

Concordantly—In agreement or harmony.

Concrete—Concentrated ; one whole.

Corporeity—The state of having a body.

Culminating—Ending ; rising to the vertical point.

David Hume—A Scottish philosopher and historian.   Born, Edinburgh 1711 ; died, 1776.

Diagnosis—Art of distinguishing ; discrimination of disease.

Digest—To dissolve and separate.

Dilution—Action by which a dose of medicine is diminished in strength.

Dilutions—Mixtures made weaker.

Druidesses—Ancient British Prophetesses.

En rapport—In sympathy, or connection with.

Entity—A separate being.

Epilepsy—An inflammatory disease.

Epitomised—Condensed ; brought into smaller compass.

Erysipelas—An inflammatory disease of the skin.

Esprit philosophique—Philosophical spirit.

Essenes—A philosophical sect.

Exstasis—Ecstasy.

External—Outward ; outside.

Faculty—Power ; virtue.

Ferrous, or Ferruginous—Composed of iron.

Flouted—Jeered at ; scorned.

Focal apparatus—Central machinery.

Ganglionic system—The great sympathetic system of nerves.

Gaul—France.

Hahnemann—The father of Homœopathy.

Hæmoglobin—A principal constituent of the blood.

Hereditary—Inherited from progenitors.

Hippocrates—Born, B.C. 460.   A founder of Medical Science.

Homœopathy—Medical doctrine of Hahnemann, *viz.*, " Like cures like."

Hypnotism—Mesmerism ; animal magnetism.

Iamblicus—Celebrated neo-Platonist of the 4th century.

Idiosyncrasy—A particular peculiarity.

Incidentally—Casually; not premeditated.

Induced—Brought about.

Infinitesimal—Exceedingly small.

Infinitude—Boundless immensity.

Inorganic—Not having organical parts.

Insulated—Isolated.

Intersecting—Mutually crossing ; dividing.

Internal—Inner.
Intervention—Interference.
Introvision—A seeing into.
Intuition—Mental insight.
Inversion—Turning inside out.
Inverted—Reversed.
Kluge—A German author.
Lamen—A table used by occultists.
Lucid—Clear.
Lucidity—Clairvoyance, or clear-sight.
Magnetoid—Magnetic.
Manganese—An oxidised metal.
Mesmer—Modern apostle of Mesmerism in Europe.
Microcosm—A miniature or little world.
Mirabile dictu—Wonderful to be told.
Modus operandi—Method of working.
Monadial—Simple, primary, atomic.
Mundane—Earthly.
Negative—Containing the least ; not so strong as the positive.
Nerve plexuses—Network of nerves.
Noxious—Harmful.
Objective—That which we know.
Oxide—Oxygen deposit.
Palliation—That which excuses or conceals.
Paracelsus—A renowned ancient physician and philosopher.
Paradox—Contrary to ; a seeming contradiction.
Par excellence—By way of eminence.
Passivity—Not opposing.
Platina—A highly valuable silver-like metal.
Pliny—Famous learned Roman Natural Historian.
Pluto and Proserpina—King and Queen of the Infernal Regions.
Polarity—Opposite properties or powers, as North and South.
Positive—Absolute ; containing the most.
Precipitate—A powdery deposit.
Promulgated—To make generally known.
Psychologists—Students of psychology.
Psychometry—Examining of substances through higher intuition.
Pythagoras—A great ancient philosopher, born about B.C. 570.
Randolph, P. B.—A famous occultist and writer of America.
Ratiocinate—To reason ; argue.
Reactivity—Action of resistance to a power applied.

Reciprocal—Interchanging.

Refraction—Rebound of rays of light.

Reichenbach (Baron v.)—Famous German optician and author.

Remote—Distant ; far off.

Resuscitation—Revival.

Salivation—Superabundant secretion of saliva.

Seer—A Clairvoyant, or Prophet.

Sensuous—Relating to the enjoyment by the senses.

Sir Charles Bell—A famous British anatomist and author.

Species—Form, appearance ; a group or kind.

Specific—Special.

Specularii—Name of an Irish sect.

Speculum—Instrument for examining cavities.

Sphere—A globe or ball.

Spontaneously—Of own accord ; voluntarily.

Stethoscope—Instrument for examining the chest.

Strabo—Ancient Geographical writer.

Striated—Marked with small channels or grooves.

St. Augustine—A famous early Father, and Missionary.

St. Justin—Celebrated Platonic philosopher and Christian Martyr.

St. Thomas Aquinas—An early Father of the Church.

Subjective—That of which we are conscious.

Succussion—Shaking.

Suetonius—Friend of Pliny. A learned author.

Surreptitious—Obtained by stealth.

Swedborg—A wonderful philosopher and theologian. Born, 1688 ; died, London, 1772.

Symmetrically—In true form and proportion.

Tacitus—Friend of Pliny. An historian and orator.

Temperament—Dominant bodily constitution.

Tenets—Principles ; opinions held to be true.

Terrestrial—Relating to the earth.

Tetragrammaton—The Lord of Hosts.

The " Call"—Invocation to a spirit.

Therapeutic—Treating disease.

Torpor—Incapability of motion ; numbness; lethargic sleep.

Transmutation—Changing of one substance into another.

Trituration—Rubbing, grinding, or reducing to powder.

Van Helmont—Paracelsian discoverer in chemistry.

Venous—The dark portal blood.

Vito-magnetic—Bodily magnetism connected with the life power.

BIBLIOGRAPHY.

Aubrey. Miscellanies. 1671.

Barrett (F.). The Magus. 1801.

Binet (A.) et Féré (C.). Animal Magnetism. 1887.

Boisardus (S.). De Divinatione per Crystallum. 16—

Crowe (Mrs.). The Seeress of Prevorst. 12mo. 1845.

Dee (John). A true and faithful relation of what passed for many years between J. D. and some spirits. 1659.

Eckhartshausen. Key to Magic. 1791.

Esdaile (J.), M.D. Natural and Mesmeric Clairvoyance.

Hartmann (Franz). Life of Paracelsus. 8vo. 1887.

Kardec (Allan). Experimental Spiritism (translated from the French by A. Blackwell). 8vo. 1876.

———— Instructions pratiques sur les manifestations Spirites. 12mo. Paris, 1858.

Lane (E. W.). Modern Egyptians. 1890.

Maury (L. F. A.). Le Magie et l'Astrologie. Paris, 1860.

Miss X. "Borderland."

Myers (F. W. H.). Phantasms of the Living. 8vo. 1886.

———— Science and a Future Life. 8vo. 1893.

"Notes and Queries." Vol. 2, p. 171, 1879; also vol. 4, 3rd series, pp. 108, 155, 218.

Paracelsus (Bombast von Hohenheim). Translation, by R. Turner, of the Supreme Mysteries of Nature; of the Spirits of the Planets; Occult Philosophy. 8vo. 1656.

———— On the Chemical Genealogy and Generation of Metals and Minerals. 8vo. 1657.

Psychical Research Society, London. Reports: Part 14, May, 1889; Part 23.

Randolph (J. B.). Seership. Toledo, Ohio, .S.A. 8vo. 1884.

Raphael's Almanacs for 1879 and 1880.

Reichenbach (Carl von, Baron). Researches on Magnetism, Crystallisation, and Chemical Attraction, in relation to Vital Force. Translator—W. Gregory. 8vo. 1850.

Stilling (Jung.) Pneumatology. 12mo. 1834.

Swedborg (E.). Various Works.

Waite (A. E.). Mysteries of Magic. 8vo. 1886.

———— Magical Writings of T. Vaughan. 8vo. 1888.

———— Occult Sciences. 8vo. 1891.

Zadkiel's Almanac for 1851.

INDEX.

	PAGE
Ancient civilisation	51, 52, 53
Angels	41
Appearances in crystal	30
Aqua-marine	7, 13
Astrology, its relations	13, 24
Beryl, Bible mention	9
—— Chaucer on the	9
—— chemical composition	9
—— colours of	7, 8, 13
—— expansion by heat	8
—— origin of name	9
—— specific gravity of	7
—— where found	8, 13
Bibliography	91
Bile	18, 23
Blood, arterial	17
—— iron in	17
—— purity of	16
—— venous	17
Brain and lung power	80
—— "centres" of "concentration"	15, 23
—— "ideality"	20
—— its poles	24, 75
—— Phrenology	15, 20
—— sight	15
—— "spirituality"	20
—— system	75
Breathing, importance of deep, to Clairvoyants	18, 80, 81

PAGE

Case of plum-stone in the duodenum - - - - - - - 69
—— of warning against dog-bite - - - - - - 72
Cerebellum a reservoir of magnetism - - - - - - 15
—— its functions - - - - - - - - - 16
—— location of - - - - - - - - - 16
Chrysoberyl - - - - - - - - - - 8
Chrysolyte - - - - - - - - - - - 8
Chrysoprasus - - - - - - - - - - 8
Clairvoyance, advantages of - - - - - - 73, 79
—— and health - - - - - - - - - 71
—— bodily diagnosis by - - - - - - - 80
—— degrees of - - - - - - - - 56, 57, 84
—— experiments with Metals - - - - - - 71
—— hereditary - - - - - - - - - 71
—— in paralysis - - - - - - - - 64
—— kinds of - - - - - - - - 56, 57, 84
—— mode of inducing by the magnet - - - - - 80
—— mode of inducing by mesmerism - - - - - 81
—— perception of disease by - - - - - - 84
—— proportions of persons who can develop - - - - 84
Cleanliness, importance of - - - - - - - 83
Clouds, their indication in Crystal - - - - - - 30
Colours, their indication in Crystal - - - - - - 30
Concentration, its importance - - - - - - 14, 15, 23
Crystal-gazing, Melville's theory - - - 14, 17, 18, 20, 23
Crystal, formation of - - - - - - - - 10
—— growth of - - - - - - - - - 11
—— magnetisation of - - - - - - - - 29
—— number of regular forms of - - - - - 12
—— refraction - - - - - - - - - 9
—— visions, classes of - - - - - - - 18, 19
Crystallomancy - - - - - - - - - 7

Dark persons, their magnetism - - - - - - 17, 30
Darkness, effect of, in clairvoyance - - - - - - 81
—— in the crystal - - - - - - - - 25
Degree, clairvoyant - - - - - - - - 57
—— extasis or trance - - - - - - - 57
—— extrovision - - - - - - - - - 57

PAGE

Degree, half-sleep - - - - - - - - - - . 56
—— introvision - - - - - - - - - - 57
—— magnetic - - - - - - - - - - - 56
—— somnambulistic - - - - - - - - - - 57
—— waking - - - - - - - - - - - 56
Derivation of name " crystal " - - - - - - - - 7
Diet in clairvoyance - - - - - - - - - - 83
Drinking, remedy for excessive - - - - - - - . 70
Drugs, their aura - - - - - - - - - - 77

Emerald, the - - - - - - - - - - 9
Epileptic fits - - - - - - - - - - 67, 68
Exhaustion - - - - - - - - - - - 70
Exstasis - - - - - - - - - - - 70
External - - - - - - - - - - - 75
Eyes, and refractive law - - - - - - - - - 8, 9
—— relation to the cerebellum - - - - - - - - 23
—— relation to the renal system - - - - - - - 23
—— their aura - - - - - - - - - - 15
—— their use in crystal-gazing - - - - - - - 29

Faces and scenes reproduced - - - - - - - 18, 19, 20
Fasting, effect on the white corpuscles - - - - - 17, 83
—— its relation to lucid sight - - - - - - - 17, 83
Fathers, the early, and crystal - - - - - - - 10, 11
Form, its brain localisation - - - - - - - - 19
—— Phrenological faculty of - - - - - - - - 19
—— relation to mental, visual - - - - - - - 19
—— reproduction - - - - - - - - - 19

Gall, Dr. - - - - - - - - - - - 19
Ganglionic system - - - - - - - - - . 75
Glossary - - - - - - - - - - - 85

Health - - - - - - - - - - 60, 71, 83

" *Ideality*," faculty of - - - - - - - - - 29
Illustrations of clairvoyance - - - - - - - - 62

PAGE

Instinct - - - - - - - - - - - . 76
Internality - - - - - - - - - - 51, 75
Introduction to clairvoyance - - - - - - 51
Intuition - - - - - - - - - - - 23
Inverted polarity - - - - - - - - - 78
Invisible beings - - - - - - - - - 65, 70
Iron and the Loadstone - - - - - - - - 17
—— approximate quantity - - - - - - - 17
—— contained in the bile - - - - - - - 18
—— contained in the Crystal - - - - - - 10
—— in human blood - - - - - - - - - 18
—— peroxide - - - - - - - - - - 17
—— protoxide - - - - - - - - - - 17
Irritability - - - - - - - - - - - 76

Jonson, Ben - - - - - - - - - - 12

Kardec, Allan - - - - - - - - - - 10
Kidneys, the Human - - - - - - - - 16, 23

Laws, principal magnetic - - - - - - - 24
" Libra," zodiacal sign, and intuition - - - - 23
Liver, Iron in the - - - - - - - - 18
Loadstone and the blood - - - - - - - . 18
—— its constituents - - - - - - - - 18

Magnetic attraction and repulsion - - - - - 62
—— discs - - - - - - - - - - 64
—— growth of Crystal - - - - - - - 11
Magnetism and Spirits - - - - - - - - 65
Manganese, its effects - - - - - - - 68, 69
Materialism - - - - - - - - - - 59
Metals, experiments with - - - - - - - 63
Mid-day - - - - - - - - - - - 40
Moon, her connection with Crystal - - - - - 14
—— her influence - - - - - - - - 25
Moonlight, effect of, on Crystal - - - - - 31
" Mugwort" Herb - - - - - - - - 20, 24

PAGE

Neck, the Human - - - - - - - - - 24
Nickel, action on Throat and Eyes - - - - - - 66, 67, 68

Operator and Crystal - - - - - - - - - 31
Oyster as a remedy - - - - - - - - 67

Paralysis - - - - - - - - - 64
Pentacles - - - - - - - - - - 35
Perceptive faculties - - - - - - - - 24, 76
Persons best adapted to Crystal-gazing - - - - - 15
Phrenology, its localisations - - - - - - 19, 68, 74
Physical love and the Cerebellum - - - - - 15
—— polarisation - - - - - - - - 75
Planets ruling "Taurus" and "Libra" - - - - - 23
Pliny, views of - - - - - - - - 9, 10
Poles of Body and Brain - - - - - - - 75
Pope, the poet - - - - - - - - 61
Prayers used by ancient Crystal-gazers - - - 25, 32, 33, 36, 39
Psychical Research Society - - - - - - 10
Purity, importance of - - - - - - 14, 15, 16

Refraction, authorities on - - - - - - - 8, 9
Religious recognition of spirit existence - - - 10, 11, 54, 73
Romans, their use of the Beryl - - - - - 13, 52
Rules for use of the Crystal - - - - - - 25, 30
—— for Clairvoyants generally - - - - - - 80, 81

Saint Augustine - - - - - - - - - 10
Spectacles - - - - - - - - - 9
Specularii, the . - - - - - - - - 9
"Spirituality," faculty of - - - - - - 20, 21
Spiritual school - - - - - - - - 61
Sunlight, effect of, on Magnetism - - - - - 31
Sunrise and use of Crystal - - - - - - 40
Sunset and use of Crystal - - - - - - 40
Swedborg, his mention of the Crystal - - - - 12
Sympathy - - - - - - - - - 77

"Taurus," the zodiacal sign - - - - - - - 24

PAGE

Temperament of " Libra " -   23
—— Moon ·   23
—— " Taurus " -   23
—— the human body   30
—— Venus ·   23

Venus and her magnetism -   30

Waite, A. E., his views   10
Water and human magnetism   19, 77

" X.," Miss, her articles on the Crystal in " Borderland "   18